DIAGNOSING

DYSLEXIA

...dults

LEEDS COLLEGE

Cynthia Klein

The Basic Skills Agency

Acknowledgement

This book was written and produced by Cynthia Klein as part of an ALBSU National Development Project in Developing Learning Support for Students with Specific Learning Difficulties (now the Basic Skills Agency). It is based on the methodology and materials developed by the Language and Literacy Unit.

The Project was based at
The Language and Literacy Unit
South Bank University
103 Borough Road
London
SE1 0AA
Telephone 020 7815 6290

The author would like to acknowledge the contributions of all the project participants and London colleagues whose comments, questions and suggestions helped to clarify points and fill gaps in the diagnostic methodology in this book.

I wish especially to thank Jenny Macwhinnie, Liz Fannin, Robin Millar, Ellen Morgan and Ann Hodgson for their contributions to the development of these materials, Anna Bramble and my co-worker on the Project Marysia Krupska for their invaluable comments and ideas and Sue Collett and Sandra Blackmore for typing this book.

ISBN 1 870741 71 7

Design: Studio 21

First edition published March 1993

Reprinted July 1995 – September 1997 – March 2000

Contents

Introduction

The purpose of this book is to offer tutors in adult, further and higher education materials for diagnosing students with specific learning difficulties (dyslexia), and thus to provide information for setting up an appropriate individualised teaching programme and making recommendations for supporting such students.

Specific learning difficulties is the term most commonly accepted by educationalists and is used in Education Acts.

Dyslexia is more commonly used within medical or neurological contexts as well as colloquially; whereas specific learning difficulties is only used in an educational context. Dyslexia is also classified as a disability by the Department of Employment.

In this book both terms are used interchangeably to refer to written language processing difficulties affecting visual, auditory and/or motor processing in reading, writing and spelling.

The materials and methods of the book can be used with students from basic literacy level to advanced level.

Materials for diagnosing beginning or non readers and writers are not included, although an interview with the student may give the tutor an *indication* of the kinds of difficulties the student is having. For non-readers and writers a period of tuition is usually advisable, whereby the tutor can observe the student's learning and through practice and discussion with the student, identify areas of weakness and strength. Other materials and approaches may be used with beginners for diagnostic purposes but these are beyond the scope of this book.

The Aims of Diagnosis

An educational diagnosis is an integral part of determining a student's educational needs. Many adults and young people in further and adult education have never had their specific difficulties diagnosed at school and have therefore absorbed confused and confusing messages about their ability to learn. To become successful learners, therefore, they need to understand their difficulties and the implication of these for learning.

Tutors and lecturers also may be confused by the dyslexic student whose consistent underachievement seems due to what may look like laziness, carelessness or inability to handle course content. Understanding a student's specific difficulties and how these may affect the student's classroom performance can enable the tutor or lecturer to adopt teaching methods and strategies to help the dyslexic student to succeed.

5

Examination boards, higher education institutions and professional bodies make various provision for students with specific learning difficulties, primarily of extra time and sympathetic consideration for spelling, handwriting and written expression difficulties. Consideration for spelling and writing difficulties is not given in English, however.

GCSE and A level boards require a report from an educational psychologist but an educational psychologist's accompanying letter with a trained learning support tutor's report is sometimes acceptable*. A trained support tutor's report is usually accepted for internal examinations such as BTEC. Other bodies will often accept a support tutor's report if it is thorough and detailed.

Methodology

The diagnostic methodology is based on the best good practice offered by current thinking and knowledge. Standardised tests are not used as they are rarely standardised beyond the age of 17 or 18 and so are not reliable for adults. Nor are reading and spelling ages used as they are demeaning and humiliating to students and give little indication as to the *kind* of difficulty and its *effects* on the student's reading, writing and spelling.

Consequently, the methodology aims for a *qualitative* analysis of difficulties, rather than a quantitative one. Not only does this give more information about the student's difficulties, but it is more appropriate to the *nature* of specific learning difficulties, which are both *individual* and persistent at *all levels* of literacy. Thus, students in higher education may continue to reveal such difficulties although they can cope with advanced reading and writing demands when given ample time and helped to develop appropriate strategies for study.

The methodology includes:

- an in-depth interview including a learning history and profile of areas of difficulty

- a miscue analysis of reading, including reading style and comprehension and reinforced by single word testing

- a spelling error analysis from a diagnostic dictation

- an analysis of a piece of free writing.

It is advisable that a student receive a period of appropriate tuition before the diagnosis; and if necessary, a period of time working with the student to observe the student's difficulties and learning style after the diagnosis may clarify the nature of the difficulties.

Although guidelines are given for using materials in this book, a period of training is recommended for making full and accurate use of these materials.

* A support tutor seeking to gain special examination provision for students with specific learning difficulties should be thoroughly trained in the theory of specific learning difficulties and methodology of diagnosis and teaching approaches.

1 | Guide to Diagnostic Assessment

The aims of the diagnostic assessment are to determine:

1. Whether or not the student's difficulties are specific learning difficulties (dyslexia) in their nature.

2. The student's strengths and weaknesses (auditory, visual, motor).

3. How these are manifested in reading, writing, spelling and attendant problems.

4. Recommendations for helping the student.

The *procedure* involves an in-depth interview, a miscue analysis of reading, including reading style and comprehension, an analysis of a piece of free writing and spelling dictation.

Preparation for the assessment includes establishing reasons for the referral and preparing the student for the diagnosis.

Reasons for the referral should be explored with the referring tutor or other referring person to determine the appropriateness of the referral. Observations by experienced teachers can be very instructive, and can be useful later if they are involved in subsequent teaching. Indicators of the likelihood of a specific learning difficulty include a discrepancy between students' evident oral abilities and their written language performance, the persistence of difficulties in acquiring the skills of reading, writing and/or spelling and other patterns of difficulty in learning which might suggest language processing problems.

The student should be well prepared for the diagnosis so it is important that the person referring explains the purpose of the diagnosis and the reasons for it. It can be distressing if the student is not clear about the purpose and reasons for the diagnosis. The student should be a *full participant* in the entire process.

The tutor doing the diagnosis should explain to the student exactly what the procedure consists of and talk through any anxieties or uncertainties the student may have, for example about reading aloud. It is also useful if the student is asked to bring a piece of writing done without the use of a dictionary and, if appropriate, a piece of writing done as a course assignment.

2 | The Diagnostic Interview

An in-depth interview forms the basis of the diagnosis. Adults can often give detailed descriptions of their difficulties, such as memorising, sequencing and fine motor co-ordination. This makes it unnecessary to give batteries of tests.

Observations of the student's use of language and expression can also inform the diagnosis; for example, word retrieval problems or difficulties pronouncing polysyllabic words may be evident.

The following is a guide to the use of the interview pro forma.

a) Current Information

Ask the student to write her name and address and observe writing style and any difficulties.

Ask about previous courses to determine whether the student has been making efforts for some years to develop written language proficiency.

Ask about educational aims to get a picture of the student's goals so the results of the diagnosis can be discussed in light of these.

Ask about student's and teachers' attitudes – i.e. how do they perceive the problem? What sort of comments do teachers make or have they made in the past? This often reveals labelling which the student has internalized, e.g. 'I was lazy/I didn't try hard enough', when in fact the student may have put in a great deal of effort.

b) Schooling

Early problems with reading and/or spelling often indicate the long-term nature and persistence of problems. Some students started off reading all right, but fell behind at a later stage. Whether or not they had extra help and whether it *did* in fact help can point to the need for *different* strategies and *specialist* help related to specific difficulties (which they may not have received).

c) Background/History

Establish the history of the student's language learning:

- What other factors could explain current problems?

- If the student is bilingual or multilingual, were there any problems in the first language? Was the student literate in the first language, and to what level?

Experience with adults often reveals that there may well be other factors in the student's background to which her difficulties have always been ascribed, and to which the student too has always ascribed them. However this does not mean that language processing difficulties are not *also* present and underachievement can sometimes be due to unidentified specific learning difficulties.

Establish any physical impairment of eyes, ears, speech, language or motor co-ordination, now or as a child. Look for:

- glue ear or frequent ear infections or colds from ages 3-7

- 'lazy eye' or squint, or history of eye-patching

- speech problems or 'late talker'

- problems learning to tie shoelaces or catching a ball.

A history of any of these can suggest the establishment of confused or inefficient perceptual or motor processing even if the physical problem no longer exists.

Dyslexia seems to be hereditary so often members of the family have similar difficulties with reading, spelling, memorising, etc.

Other signs can be an at-risk or difficult birth, or a history of respiratory or neurological prolems.

d) Language/Listening Behaviours

Establish *undue* difficulty with auditory or auditory-motor processing skills.

Word retrieval is important; slowness in 'naming' or 'finding' words seems to be a common factor among many dyslexic people.

Give examples of multisyllabic words to pronounce, e.g. preliminary, anemone, contemporaneous.*

e) Student's Description of Reading

First identify the student's reading level by finding out what she reads: e.g. newspapers – which ones and which bits, magazines, stories, novels, course or work related texts. Does she read a lot or very little?

Try to get a sense from the student's experience of reading whether any difficulty is one of comprehension, slowness, tracking the print, visual stress or recognising words, which may indicate a visual processing difficulty; or whether it is more a problem of poor decoding or phonetic attack, which may suggest auditory processing difficulties. It is also useful to explore students' approaches to reading: e.g. do they need dim light or a quiet place, but also do they try to sound out words or guess from context?

* from the Bangor Dyslexia Test

f) Student's Description of Spelling and Writing Problems

Again, try to determine the appropriate level of writing and spelling; often in dyslexic adults there is a considerable discrepancy between reading level and spelling level. Try to get a sense of the student's experience of writing and understanding of the writing process. Most dyslexic students experience great difficulty getting ideas onto paper, finding the 'right' words and organising their ideas.

Inconsistency is an important clue (like electrical impulses which sometimes connect and sometimes do not).

Inability to proof read can suggest a poor visual memory of a word against which to match an attempt.

g) Maths

This is included to give a full picture; some dyslexic students are good at maths, others have difficulty with memorising tables or formulae, transposing figures, arithmetic inaccuracies. They may have especial difficulties with aspects of maths which require many steps or place a heavy load on the short-term memory, e.g. long division or algebra. Some do impressive and creative calculations to compensate for a poor memory for number facts.

h) Memorisational Difficulties

Memorisation difficulties particularly relate to sequences such as the alphabet and months of the year; students may have had trouble in the past, or still have problems. Often, if they have learned the alphabet they cannot tell where a letter is in the sequence without going back to the beginning. Look to see if they are particularly dependent on meaning and cannot learn by rote.

Sometimes students are not fully aware of their memorisational difficulties or difficulties with sequence, so in such a case it can be useful to ask them to show you; for example to recite the alphabet or months of the year, to ask what letter comes after 'n', to recite the 7 x table or to repeat a sequence of three or four numbers forwards and then backwards.

It also helps to find out what techniques they do use if they want to remember something (e.g. something for their course) – is it more visual, auditory, motor? They may also use more 'right brain' strategies, such as imagery or rhythm. Assess if they seem to have to work particularly hard at this. Storing, retrieving and coordinating facts and information are usually problematic.

Students may be pleased to have achieved success in some of these areas: look for whether they had *undue* difficulty in doing so.

i) Spatial/Temporal

This section contains specific cues to get students to reflect on the nature of any spatial and/or temporal difficulties. These are used to corroborate other findings. Students may give their own examples which it is helpful to note verbatim.

Difficulty following directions can indicate short-term auditory memory problems and difficulties with sequences. It may be useful to give a hypothetical example. Giving the student instructions such as 'point to my right ear with your left hand' can sometimes reveal difficulties.

Difficulty learning to tell the time may indicate a temporal problem or may be a directional one of transposing the clock face. Some students find they still have these difficulties and can only use a digital watch.

Even if a student has mastered these difficulties now, look for indications of whether it was a struggle to do so.

j) Visual-Motor

Look for evidence of motor co-ordination problems. These may be very fine motor co-ordination problems, sometimes only exhibited in written language. Also, note any description by the student which suggests confused motor control or lack of motor integration, e.g. the student intends to write one word but finds his or her hand writing another, 'hand adds or writes letters with a mind of its own', hand tires easily, student has to press hard to control pen or think about forming the letters. Also observe the way the student holds the pen and paper while writing to note any extreme degree of rotation or peculiarity of pen grip.

SPECIFIC LEARNING DIFFICULTIES

Diagnostic Interview

Student's Name: .... Date: ....

Address: ....

....

....

Telephone: .... Age (if relevant): ....

College/Institution: ....

Contact: ....

Course/Work Information: ....

Considerations requested:

☐ examinations ☐ extra time

☐ sympathetic consideration ☐ extra time in assignments

☐ other (specify)

Other college/educational experiences since leaving school: ....

....

Educational aims of student: ....

....

Attitude of teachers: ....

....

Attitude of student/self-assessment of difficulties: ....

....

Schooling-primary

☐ problems learning to read ☐ received extra help

☐ second language interference ☐ disruptions/missed school

Comments: ....

Schooling-secondary

- ☐ problems recognised by school
- ☐ extra help
- ☐ exams attempted (particularly English)
- ☐ exams passed/grades
- ☐ consideration given

Comments: ....

Background/history

- ☐ ear infections/'glue ear' (primary school)
- ☐ vision problems: squint/lazy eye/other
- ☐ motor coordination problems (e.g. tying shoelaces/catching a ball or 'clumsy child' syndrome)
- ☐ speech or language difficulties/'late talker'
- ☐ other members of family have similar difficulties
- ☐ any serious health problems, e.g. respiratory, neurological

Comments: ....

Language/listening behaviours

- ☐ trouble listening
- ☐ trouble concentrating with background noise
- ☐ pronunciation difficulties, especially with multi-syllabic words
- ☐ word retrieval problems
- ☐ problems with listening and taking notes simultaneously

Comments: ....

Reading

Approximate level:

- ☐ needs to re-read frequently
- ☐ comprehension difficulties
- ☐ word recognition problems
- ☐ decoding problems
- ☐ oral reading difficulties
- ☐ problems tracking print
- ☐ print 'dances', blurs or irritates eyes

Approaches used by student:

Comments: ....

Writing and Spelling

Approximate level:

☐ difficulty getting ideas down on paper

☐ word retrieval problems

☐ problems with grammar/sentence structure/punctuation

☐ problems with organisation and planning

Planning strategies used:

☐ 'good' days and 'bad' days

☐ difficulties remembering what words look like

☐ difficulties discriminating/'holding' sounds

General spelling approaches used by student:

Comments: ....

Maths

☐ difficulties memorizing times tables

☐ difficulties memorizing basic number facts

☐ general proficiency

☐ difficulties with long division/algebra, etc

☐ other (specify):

General approach:

Comments: ....

Memorisational difficulties

☐ alphabet

☐ months/days/seasons

☐ telephone numbers

☐ erratic memory

☐ names, dates, factual information

☐ other (specify)

Strategies used:

Comments: ....

Spatial/temporal

- ☐ difficulties learning to tell time
- ☐ left/right confusions
- ☐ gets lost easily

- ☐ map reading difficulties
- ☐ difficulties following oral directions
- ☐ other (specify)

Comments: ....

Visual-motor

- ☐ copying difficulties
- ☐ letter reversals
- ☐ unusual paper position
- ☐ unusual pen grip
- ☐ left-handed

- ☐ difficulties controlling pen
- ☐ irregular or awkward letter construction
- ☐ problems with writing what's intended/ much crossing out, etc
- ☐ hand gets tired after short period of writing

Other information:

3 | Reading

The second stage of the diagnostic assessment after the interview is to analyse the student's reading through a miscue analysis of oral reading, followed by the student's retelling of the passage and specific comprehension questions. Single words and non-words may also be given to the student to read in order to inform the analysis.

The aim of the analysis is to determine the nature and extent of the student's difficulties with reading. However, in order to do this, it is important that the tutor be clear about the nature of the reading process and the way in which proficient readers read. Many theories and assumptions about reading abound and can influence the tutor's perception of the reader's difficulties. For example, a student who relies heavily on context to work out words but has good comprehension may be perceived as having no reading problems. On closer look, however, such a student may be struggling with unfamiliar words, and may be unable to tackle words out of context. *Having* to rely on context is a handicap, not a sign of a competent reader; the latter can rapidly read single words in any context, even the most unexpected.

On the other hand, readers may read a passage with little or no apparent difficulty and again be perceived as having no reading problems. Whereas, if comprehension is then tested, some students may be seen to have understood little of what they read.

For a full discussion of the reading process and how dyslexia may affect readers, see 'The Reading Process' in the Appendix.

SELECTING A READING PASSAGE

In selecting a reading passage it is necessary to select a passage at the right level in order both to generate errors and to assess students' reading skills in relation to the demands of their jobs or courses.

Through the interview, the tutor should find out what sort of reading the student does both for pleasure and for work or study in order to try to assess the student's level. A passage can be selected from course work but should be an unfamiliar passage and should be long and complex enough to reveal any comprehension problems. It should also be difficult enough to reveal the student's strategies for dealing with unknown words and accessing and monitoring meaning.

It can be useful to do a readability analysis of the passage using Fogg or Smog or any similar method. The Fogg readability formula is included here. There are many criticisms of readability methods but they can be helpful as a guide to the level of reading material. It is important, however, to use the 'reading age' from such an analysis *only* as a guide to the difficulty of the passage and *not* as a reading age for the student.

One of the problems with assessing the reading of a more advanced student is that the student's difficulties may not show up with a passage which is relatively easy, whereas significant problems may occur with a more difficult passage. If students are struggling with the reading on a course, it is important to identify the kind of problems they will encounter in the course of study.

However, the passage should not be so difficult for the student that she cannot recognise or work out enough words to make sense of the passage; if the struggle seems too great, try an easier passage! This book contains a selection of reading passages at different levels which may be used or may act as examples regarding length and level of difficulty for choosing your own.

MISCUE ANALYSIS

Miscue Analysis is a tool for looking closely at the types of strategies a reader uses as she reads. It was devised by an American educationalist, Kenneth Goodman, and is based upon psycholinguistic theory. Its aim is to observe how well the reader processes visual material in the search for meaning and how fluent, regardless of the reading level, her reading is.

'Goodman coined the word "miscue" in the 1960's to describe any departure the reader makes from the actual words of the text . . . Goodman's purpose in coining this term "miscue" was twofold:– First, he wanted to get away from the notion that every departure from the words of the text is necessarily bad, something to be considered an error. Second, he wanted to emphasize how such departures from the text indicated which language cue systems the reader is using and not using, at least at the particular moment; the pattern of miscues thus suggests the reader's strengths as well as weaknesses . . .' (Weaver, 1988).

The aim of miscue analysis is to examine miscues 'from a point of view of how close they are to what had been expected' in order to identify 'the pattern of a reader's strengths and weaknesses. These patterns may reveal linguistic or conceptual weaknesses' . . . or may show how a reader who 'repeats words and phrases, miscues and corrects, is deeply and actively processing printed material for meaning.' ('The Aims of Miscue Analysis', source unknown).

The Cueing Systems

There are three major cueing systems which the reader can use in reading a text:

Grapho/phonic cues: *letter/sound* cues, i.e. visual analysis of letter patterns/the correspondences between letters (graphemes) and sounds (phonemes).

Semantic cues: *meaning* cues from each sentence, both forward and backward, and from the whole as the reader progresses.

Syntactic cues: grammatical cues including word order, grammatical endings, function words and sentence structure.

1. The Grapho/phonic System

The grapho/phonic system may be seen as two subsystems: one of visual whole word recognition or analysis of visual patterns and the other of the correspondence between letters and sounds. Although Goodman, Frank Smith and others in the 1960's and 1970's put forward the theory that the skilled reader uses a minimum of visual cues, only enough to *predict* a word, recent research suggests that the skilled reader reads *primarily* from rapid word recognition based on rapid visual analysis with reference to an internal lexicon. The phonic or 'sounding out' route is used by the skilled reader primarily when confronted with an unfamiliar word.

The learner reader may go through a phase of relying on the phonic route to 'crack the code' but by the reading age of eight, receptiveness to visual cues is dominating the reading process (Marie Clay, 1985). Over-reliance on the phonic route may suggest difficulties in recognising familiar words. If the student is not monitoring for meaning and is making nonsense or non-word miscues, then she is over-relying on the grapho/phonic system.

On the other hand, if the miscues show poor visual or phonic resemblance, then the student may have a weakness in the grapho/phonic system. Often students are able to use initial letters but show a weakness in decoding or recognising endings or middles. Such students will often have to compensate by relying more on semantic and syntactic cues.

2. The Semantic System

This system provides information about the appropriateness of meaning given by the context of a word. For example, the sentence 'They refurnished their house' read as 'They refurnished their home' would show that the reader has kept the meaning largely intact. However, the sentence read as 'They refurnished their horse' shows a weakness in the use of the semantic system. The skilled reader monitors for meaning both reading ahead and reading back. For example in the following sentences, 'She wanted to sell her house. She hoped someone would be happy living in it,' a substitution of 'horse' for 'house' makes sense for the first sentence but not when you add the second. A reader who makes such miscues is not reading ahead to monitor meaning.

3. The Syntactic System

This system provides information about grammatical appropriateness. Language is rule-governed, and intuitive knowledge of grammatical structures and conventions is part of knowing a language. Grammatical structures limit the possible choices a reader can make. A reader who is not a native English speaker or who has certain types of linguistic weaknesses may not be able to use this system fully. On the other hand they may adapt what they read to their 'own' grammar. For instance, a typical Londoner might read 'We were all at the pub last night' as 'We *was* all at the pub last night'. This adapting of grammar or vocabulary is part of what a skilled reader does in getting meaning from a text and does *not* show poor use of the syntactic system. An example of poor use of this system would be reading the sentence. 'His eyes were small and deep set' as 'His eyes were small and deep *sit*".

Procedure

Miscue Analysis is not a *test* but a way of obtaining an overall picture of the student's strengths and weaknesses in reading. It should be shared with the student so that the student fully understands its purpose and how it can lead to more effective strategies for learning and teaching by identifying the student's strengths and weaknesses.

Select a passage for the student to read aloud. It should be slightly above the student's reading level, of moderate difficulty. It should generate 20-25 miscues to reveal a pattern of difficulty. Photocopy the passage for yourself to mark up. Taping the student is helpful as it means that you can mark up the passage later and can concentrate on observing the reader, but with experience you may not need to use a tape.

Explain to the student why you need to hear her read aloud, so that you can see how she reads and what kind of difficulties she is having.

Suggest that the student look over the passage first and begin reading when ready. Tell the student to read for meaning as you will ask her to tell you about what she read. Tell the student not to worry about difficulties and to feel free to pause, read bits over and make guesses, but that you will not help because you want to see how she works the words out herself.

After the student has finished reading, remove the text and ask the student to tell you what it was about in as much detail as she can remember. Record this verbatim. Follow with some questions about significant details from the passage.

If the student is an advanced reader, she may not make enough errors. In this case an analysis of comprehension and reading style may be adequate to identify the student's strengths and weaknesses. However, it may also be useful to test the student with single word lists of regular and irregular words and non-words.

Marking System

Errors can be recorded in different ways, but the following chart includes the most useful symbols. (Chart adapted from M. Walsh, June 1979).

Miscue	Symbol	
Non-response	_work _	Use a broken line to indicate an inability or refusal to attempt a word.
Substitution	*play* / work	Write substituted word above appropriate part of text.
Insertion	*his* / for ∧ work	Indicate by insertion sign, and write inserted word above.
Omission	(work)	Circle word, words or parts of words omitted.
Repetition	work	Underline words repeated.
Correction	*play* © / work	Place a small © beside corrected word. (MC) for miscorrection.
Reversal	work \ hard / o \ n	Symbol that shows which parts of letters, words, phrases, or clauses have been interchanged.
Hesitation	work / hard / work // hard	Hesitation between two words. Extra long hesitation.

It is also useful to use (v) for language variety for a miscue which is the result of the reader using non-Standard English grammar.

In recording non-word substitutions, spelling should reflect grapho/phonic cues that the reader is using. For example, if a reader reads 'phenomena' as fu-hon-ma, it should be spelled above the original as 'phuhonma' to show that the reader is using the 'ph' as a cue.

You should note repetitions and self corrections as these are signs of monitoring meaning. You should also note hesitations and other aspects of reading style (see 'Reading Style' section).

20

Analysing Miscues

The following coding system is adapted from Goodman and has been modified to aid accurate assessment of reading difficulties.

We code + for effective use of a cueing system

√ for partial use of a cueing system

o for little or no use of a cueing system

Each error is coded for all three cueing systems.

---

1. The Grapho/phonic System

How much does the miscue *look* like what was expected?
How much does the miscue *sound* like what was expected?

In most adult readers, beyond the basic literacy stage, the look of a word should predominate and for advanced readers the phonic aspect should be minimal. However, we code both columns to help observe if the student is using the immediate visual route or the mediated phonic route. In most cases these will be similar or the stronger system will be revealed by close analysis.

For example: 'heard' for 'head' would show a + for the graphic or visual cue but a √ for the phonic or sounding out, showing the reader relying on visual whole word recognition.

On the other hand: 'ajest' for 'aghast' would show a + for the phonic and a √ for the visual system. Here the reader is relying on 'sounding out' rather than visual recognition.

Grapho/phonic similarity is high (+) if most of the word (beginning, middle and end) has a high graphic similarity and/or has been decoded with a fair amount of accuracy. Non-word substitutions tend to show an over-reliance on phonic cues. To identify high graphic similarity it is useful to observe your own miscues when you read, as a rule of thumb.

Grapho/phonic similarity is partial (√) if the miscue has some graphic similarity and/or some part or parts of the word have been accurately decoded.

If there is little or no similarity or accurate decoding, then the reader shows no grapho/phonic strength (o).

Some examples of miscue with high grapho/phonic similarity:

Text	Miscue	Visual	Phonic
waist	wrist	+	✓
straightened	strengthened	+	✓
owing	owning	+	✓
promptings	promotings	+	✓
acclimatization	acclimatation	✓	+
detriment	determent	+	+

Examples of miscues with partial grapho/phonic similarity:

Text	Miscue	Visual	Phonic
present	patient	✓	✓
fortitude	fortunate	✓	✓
sedately	sadly	✓	✓
acclimatization	accumulation	✓	✓
opposite	ossopit	✓	✓

Examples of miscues with little or no grapho/phonic similarity:

Text	Miscue	Visual	Phonic
present	perched	o	o
almost	awfully	o	o
aghast	gasingly	o	o
usual	surface	o	o
flickering	blinking	o	o

2. The Semantic System

Is the miscue acceptable in relation to the meaning that the context gives a word?

Semantic strength is high when the original meaning of the sentence is relatively unchanged. Most miscues will modify the meaning to some extent, but they are highly acceptable (+) when they are close to the author's intent within the context of the whole passage.

Semantic strength is partial ($\checkmark$) when the miscue is appropriate within a single sentence or part of a sentence but not within the total context, as in the example of horse/house given earlier.

If there is no evidence of semantic acceptability, the miscue is coded as (o).

Some examples of miscues with high semantic acceptability (+):

Text	*Miscue*
violent *(explosions)*	volcanic
disruptive *(adolescent)*	destructive
(lit my) smoke	cigarette
(seemed to) afford *(him much pleasure)*	offer

Examples of partial semantic acceptability ($\checkmark$):

Text	*Miscue*
(The ill effects of altitude on the climber may at least be) retarded *(by a careful regime of . . .)*	regarded
(up on the roof the) pigeons *(were gathered)*	penguins

(The story has been describing and goes on to describe tropical creatures in a tropical setting).

Examples of poor semantic acceptability (o):

Text	*Miscue*
(Up on the roof the) pigeons *(were gathered)*	pigments
(his) owner	over
(sent him to London Zoo as a) present	parent

Non-words are always coded (o).

3. Syntactic System

Does the miscue work grammatically in the context of the sentence?

Miscues are syntactically either appropriate (+) or not appropriate (o), so there is no partial strength.

Examples of miscues which show syntactic strength (+):

Text	Miscue
(send him as a) present	patient
(he had huge) arms	hands
(if he had) straightened *(up)*	stretched
fully *(mature)*	finally

To be coded as a (+), a miscue must be a real word.

Examples which show syntactic weakness (o):

Text	Miscue
(was quite) devoid *(of hair)*	devote
(both) sides *(of his face)*	besides
(wandered about) aimlessly	airless
(a) glitter *(of ironic laughter)*	greater

Language variety (v) miscues which are appropriate to the student's spoken grammar should be coded as (+). For example, a Caribbean Creole speaker might read:

'Just about everybody likes to dance.'

(with *like* (v) written above *likes*)

Insertions and omissions can be coded to show syntactic and and semantic strengths and weaknesses.

For example:

'I was taken into a classroom with lots of other (little) boys and girls . . .'

and:

'I was never quite sure whether the telegraph-poles were very strong . . .'

(with *the* inserted at ∧)

Both show semantic and syntactic acceptability; whereas,

'Sometimes he left (after) a few days'.

changes the meaning and is syntactically weak.

24

Corrections

Corrections should be noted in the final column with a tick. They indicate that the student is monitoring meaning and should be considered as part of the student's reading style.

Final Points:

1. You are looking for an *overall pattern*.
2. This is a *tool for observation* – you need to get experience of using it and it won't give you all the answers.
3. Students may be *inconsistent* in using cueing systems.
4. You need to check *comprehension* (orally), through;
   - a summary to show spontaneous recall and sequencing
   - questions which show ability to make inferences from the text as well as give literal answers.
5. It is very important to observe *reading style* (e.g. word for word, jerky, ignoring punctuation or lots of hesitations and repetitions, etc).

Students with *(visual)* word recognition problems often rely on a phonic approach and will make non-word substitutions, frequently showing semantic weaknesses. They often ignore punctuation, read jerkily and may miss out words or lose their place. They also show few signs of monitoring comprehension (e.g. repetitions and corrections) and their comprehension is frequently vague because all their concentration is going into trying to recognise or work out the words.

Students with poor *(auditory)* phonic skills may read with good understanding but will often struggle with words they don't know, rely heavily on context and substitute whole words which show attempts to make sense. They usually make frequent repetitions and often self-correct. In spite of their difficulties, their comprehension is frequently good with spontaneous recall of significant details.

References

The Aims of Miscue Analysis (source unknown).

Marie Clay, *The Early Detection of Reading Difficulties*, 1985, (3rd edition).

Andrew Ellis, *Reading, Writing and Dyslexia*, Erlbaum, 1984.

Yetta M. Goodman and Carolyn Burke, *Reading Miscue Inventory Manual; Procedure for Diagnosis and Evaluation*, 1972.

Frank Smith, *Understanding Reading*, Erlbaum, 1971, 1978, 1982.

Philip T. Smith, 'Development of Reading: The Acquisition of a Cognitive Skill', in *Language Acquisition*, ed Paul Fletcher and Michael Garman, Cambridge University Press, 1986.

Margaret Walsh, *Miscue Analysis*, ALU Newsletter (No.5), June 1979.

Margaret Snowling, *Dyslexia: A Cognitive Developmental Perspective*, 1987.

Constance Weaver, *Reading Process and Practice*, Heinmann, 1988.

CHUMLEY

Chumley was a full-grown chimpanzee. his owner, a District Officer, was finding the ape's large size rather awkward, and he wanted to send him to London Zoo as a present, so that he could visit the animal when he was back in England on leave. He wrote asking us if we would mind taking Chumley back with us when we left, and depositing him at his new home in London, and we replied that we would not mind at all.

He arrived in the back of a small van, seated sedately in a huge crate. when the doors of his crate were opened and Chumley stepped out with all the ease and self-confidence of a film star, I was considerably shaken, for, standing on his bow legs in a normal slouching chimp position, he came up to my waist, and if he had straightened up, his head would have been on a level with my chest. He had huge arms, and must have measured at least twice my measurements round his hairy chest. Owing to bad tooth growth both sides of his face were swollen out of all proportion, and this gave him a weird pugilistic look. His eyes were small, deep-set, and intelligent the top of his head was nearly bald owing, I discovered later, to his habit of sitting and rubbing the palm of his hand backwards across his head, an exercise which seemed to afford him much pleasure and which he persisted in until the top of his skull was quite devoid of hair. This was no young chimp as I had expected, but a veteran of about eight or nine years, fully mature, strong as a powerful.

Miscue Analysis Form

Student's Name ...... Peter ......
Date ......
Reading Selection ...... Chumley ......

Script	Miscue	Grapho-phonic		Semantic	Syntactic	Corrections
		Visual	Phonetic			
Chumley	Cherrylyn	✓	o	+	+	✓
District	Director	✓	o	✓	o	✓
apes	open	✓	o	o	o	✓
present	parent	+	✓	o	+	
wrote	wote	+	✓	o	o	✓
we	he	✓	o	o	+	
his	the	o	o	+	+	✓
the	a	o	o	o	+	✓
seated	standing	o	o	✓	+	
"	sitting	✓	✓	+	+	✓
sedately	steadily	✓	o	+	+	
crate	cage	✓	o	+	+	
his	the	o	o	+	+	✓
chumley	cherrily	✓	✓	+	+	
film	fully	✓	o	o	o	✓
slouching	secluding	✓	o	o	o	
straightened	strengthened	+	✓	o	o	(mc)
"	stretched	✓	✓	+	+	
head	hand	✓	✓	✓	o	
measured	muscles	✓	o	✓	o	✓
tooth	toes	✓	o	o	o	✓
this	his	✓	✓	o	o	✓
weird	warid	+	+	o	o	
pugilistic	puglistic	✓	✓	o	o	
persisted	persided	✓	✓	✓	+	✓
skull	shin	✓	✓	o	o	
devoid	divided	✓	✓	o	o	
fully	finally	✓	✓	o	o	
as	and	✓	o	o	o	

Observations from reading:

No. of repetitions...... 14 ......

No. of corrections...... 14 ......

Observed strengths/weaknesses:

Reading style (see attached sheet):

Frequent repetitions and corrections show he is monitoring meaning. Often hesitates before difficult words/when unsure of meaning shows excellent and detailed memory of passage but his struggle with decoding words makes reading arduous.

Weakness in graph/phonic system, particularly in using phonic cues. Usually substitutes whole words but does not predict, but high numbers of corrections and repetitions shows he relies heavily on context: needs to use context better to predict.

Miscue Analysis Form

Date ....

Student's Name .... Reading Selection ....

Script	Miscue	Grapho-phonic		Semantic	Syntactic	Corrections
		Visual	Phonetic			

Observations from reading:

No. of repetitions.............................

No. of corrections.............................

Observed strengths/weaknesses:

Reading style (see attached sheet):

READING STYLE ANALYSIS

When analysing a student's reading, it is important to consider the student's reading style as a whole and in its various aspects as well as the student's comprehension as part of a miscue analysis. The aim is to draw up a profile of the reader in terms of the approach to reading, strategies used, strengths and weaknesses. It is this *whole* picture that enables an accurate analysis which can be the basis of a clear understanding of the student's difficulties and the setting up of an effective individual learning programme.

The following is a guide for drawing up such a reading profile.

Overall Style

Does student read:

- word-for-word

- jerkily

- stressing each syllable, even pitch, heavy stress

- without regard for punctuation

- fluently with hesitations only before difficult words

- pausing after phrases and whole sentences at punctuation points?

What do these tell you about the student's reading approach and difficulties?

Hesitations

Does the student make frequent or long hesitations before words or before bits of words? Hesitations show where the student has a problem – is it before unexpected words, words which the student doesn't recognise or words the student can't 'attack' or sound out?

Repetitions

Does the student repeat words/phrases/whole sentences? Frequent repetitions show the student is searching for and consolidating meaning.

Visual-motor Tracking

Does the student lose place easily, miss out words or lines, need to use a finger for tracking?

Are there examples of sequential errors? Interference of words from one line of print to the one above or below?

Corrections

Does the student correct miscues – often, occasionally, never?

Does the student seem to be monitoring meaning by self-correcting?

Does the student overcorrect, e.g. errors which do not impede or alter meaning?

Does the student miscorrect accurate reading?

Cueing Systems

What kind of cueing systems does the student seem to be using for unfamiliar words?

- letter-sound analysis
- syllables and letter clusters
- little words in bigger words
- visual analysis by analogy
- syntactic and semantic content, e.g. prediction.

Does the student seem to have limited word attack skills?

Does the student have only one way of attacking unfamiliar words, e.g. lack flexibility or the ability to use a variety of cueing systems?

Does the student:

- misread common/familiar words?
- have to rely on 'sounding-out' because of failure to recognise familiar words?

COMPREHENSION

Retelling

- Was the student able to extract main points and significant details from the text?
- How does the student relate details?
  - in the order they were given?
  - in any kind of developmental order?
  - at random?
  Are there signs of sequential or organisational difficulties?
- Can the student see inherent connections between details? Draw conclusions?
  Are problems with short-term or 'working' memory interfering with complex comprehension skills?

Specific Questions

- Do student's answers confirm retelling: are there contradictions?
- Is student able to add/focus on details which may have been omitted in the retelling?
- Do answers confirm comprehension of particular points/ability to draw conclusions or make inferences?

Language and Vocabulary

- Does the student reveal expressive language difficulties, e.g.
  - word retrieval problems
  - vocabulary confusions
  - problems saying what she means/vague use of language?
- Was vocabulary difficult or unfamiliar? (note examples)
- Is the student familiar with/does she know the meaning of words she doesn't recognise in print?

SINGLE WORD AND NONWORD TESTING

Sometimes, especially with more advanced readers who do not make enough miscues, it is helpful to use single word and nonword testing to help identify or clarify the student's particular difficulties in reading.

Three types of 'tests' are included here: The Irregular Word List, The Long Regular Word List and The Snowling Graded Nonword Test (Revised Pilot Version). The Irregular Word List is made up of irregular words, i.e. those which cannot be pronounced accurately by using phonic basic 'rules'. Instead, they need to be *recognised* in order to read them accurately. Such words are useful in helping to determine a reader's word recognition skills.

However, because these words do rely on recognition for accurate reading, the reader must *know* the words in order to read them. It is only reliable as a guide when using words which are familiar to the student. Therefore, the list should be used as a resource to select from it words appropriate to each particular student. *It is a student's difficulty in recognising familiar words that you are looking for.*

The Long Regular Word List, on the other hand, is composed of words which can be accurately 'read' by using phonic 'rules' whether the reader knows them or not, or indeed has any idea of their meaning at all. Such words can indicate the reader's ability to use a phonic strategy and to 'track' long words. Therefore, this list can be given as it is. It can be useful to compare the student's performance on the irregular and regular words; often the student is much better at one than the other. This can then inform the analysis of the student's strengths and weaknesses in reading.

However, as the long regular words are indeed *words*, a reader can read the familiar ones by recognising them. To get a more accurate picture of the student's skills in phonic attack, it can be useful to give the reader non-words to read as these can *only* be read through phonic attack. The Snowling Graded Nonword Test is therefore included for this purpose. The test is not standardised for adults so it can only be used to provide information on the reader's phonic skills. It is worth remembering, however, that a proficient reader will be able to 'read' all of these non words with no difficulty whatsoever; consequently any difficulties a student has may be illuminating.

4 | Spelling Error Analysis

Spelling error analysis is a way of analysing a student's spellings in order to identify the student's strengths and weaknesses and approach to spelling, as part of the diagnostic process.

Many adult students who have developed strategies for coping with reading continue to have considerable problems with spelling and writing which seriously affect their academic performance. A large discrepancy between the level of reading and that of spelling is one indicator of possible dyslexia, particularly when the types of errors show persistent difficulty in acquiring sounds, letter patterns and/or the conventions of English spelling.

The analysis and categorisation of errors is based on a modification of the work of Margaret Peters.

Introducing the Spelling Dictation

A piece of the student's writing which contains at least 20-25 errors is needed in order to identify a pattern of difficulty. A diagnostic dictation at the appropriate level for the student is more likely to reveal the extent and pattern of the student's difficulties than a piece of free writing where the student may avoid words she is unable to spell. Explain to the student that the dictation is not a test, but that it will help you to identify what kinds of difficulties she has and enable you to suggest the best ways of overcoming them.

Ask the student to make a best guess if she does not know how to spell some of the words. It may be helpful to explain to the student the value of guessing, that it can help you both to see exactly where her difficulties lie. If the student can appreciate the usefulness of errors, she is likely to be less anxious and feel more of a participant in the diagnostic process. Dictate the passage at a pace the student can easily follow. Tell the student that you will not put in punctuation but will expect her to do it herself. If the student has difficulty remembering, slow down or break the sentence into smaller chunks. Also tell the student she will have time afterwards to proofread for punctuation and to correct spellings if she wants.

When the dictation is completed, ask the student to read over what she has written and to underline words she thinks are wrong. The student may correct words if she thinks she can by writing the correct version above the incorrect attempt, in the margin or at the bottom of the page. This will show you if the student can 'see' her own errors. It is also useful to observe the student writing as this will show you how much time the student has to spend thinking about spellings, how 'automatic' spelling and handwriting are, and whether the student has handwriting problems such as having to press hard to control the pen, adding or omitting letters unintentionally, or having difficulty getting the hand to go in the intended direction (e.g. writing a 'd' for a 'g').

The dictations included here are from Margaret Peters and the most difficult of the three is graded for children aged 10-11. More advanced students may therefore not make enough errors on the dictation and can be given additional words from the advanced spelling list to generate more errors. (For more advanced and vocationally based dictations, see Hulley 1992).

Classifying the Errors

Check the piece of writing for errors and compare the student's spelling errors with the correct spellings using the chart.

Errors are classified in the following categories:

A. **Logical phonetic alternatives** which follow English spelling convention; i.e. they would be an 'acceptable' alternative. Examples of these errors would be *serface* for *surface*, *groops* for *groups*, *resently* for *recently*. Homonyms also fall into this category.

B. **Visual sequential errors,** i.e. usually two letters out of order, as in *Britian* for *Britain*, *claer* for *clear* and *dose* for *does*. These are errors to do with visual rather than auditory memory; signficant sounds which are missequenced, such as the *r* in *hreat* for *heart* would be categorised in column D.

C. **Rule base errors,** or those which show lack of awareness of spelling rules or are unacceptable phonetic alternatives. Examples would be *copys* for *copies*, *jocked* for *joked*, *pocet* for *pocket* (because *c* followed by *e* would be pronounced *poset*), *stashun* for *station* (because the sound *shun* is not spelled that way as a suffix), *imediatly* for *immediately*.

D. **Sounds missing, misheard or missequenced.** Sometimes they can be very disordered. Examples are *wising* for *whistling*, *kinf* for *knife*, *scelye* for *scarcely*, *sepate* for *separate*, *volient* for *violent*.

E. **Motor errors** which may take the form of handwriting errors, repetition or omission of letters, telescoping or perseverating. Examples of telescoping would be *beging* for *beginning* and *presion* for *precision*. Telescoping is visual-motor rather than auditory when the missing letters are not significant sounds, but rather repeated or similar looking and sounding letters; it shows a lack of eye-hand co-ordination. An example of perseveration would be *machinine* for *machine* where the hand repeats a letter pattern. Another type of motor error is when one word is substituted for another, i.e. the hand 'takes over' and writes another word than the one intended, for example *particular* for *peculiar*.

33

However, such substitutions are not always motor; students with auditory processing weaknesses will sometimes substitute another word because it 'looks right' (i.e. it is a real word) and they are unable to discriminate between similar sounding words. Examples of such errors are *disguise* for *discuss* and *serious* for *series;* these would be classified in Column D.

Decide how to classify each error and tick the appropriate column. Some errors may fall into more than one column, but where possible make the obvious choice. If it contains two or more errors which are classified differently, tick the one further to the *right*. This means you are categorising the most severe error. Some errors may be difficult to classify and it may be useful to hold these until the end when you can see the overall *pattern* of errors. Two students may spell a word the same way for different reasons. **Remember, it is the *overall pattern of errors* which is important.**

Interpretation of the Chart

Students may make errors of all types, but note the *frequency* with which errors fall into the different columns. Students will generally reveal a pattern, with a *predominance* of errors in one or two columns.

Column A

This column will include words which are near to the correct spelling or seem to be possible 'alternative spellings'. They show the student is close to learning appropriate combinations of letters and to integrating 'rules' for generalising English spelling patterns.

If most of the errors are in this column, the student understands spelling convention and with practice is probably on the way to becoming a successful speller. However, if these sorts of errors *persist* and the student continues to make large numbers of errors, she may have a poor visual memory and may need to develop auditory and other strategies for remembering.

Column B

A number of errors in this column indicates the student has difficulty remembering or revisualising the sequence of the letters correctly. The visual memory of the word is poor, so other strategies for remembering need to be developed.

Column C

A large number of errors in this column show that the student does not have a clear idea of which combination of letters to use. She may be making a phonetic attempt, but fails to follow English spelling convention, i.e. the word *could not* be spelled like that in English. The student probably has difficulties assimilating rules and generalising; she may need to be taught how words are built up and to link words to those of a similar pattern.

Column D

A larger number of errors here shows difficulty in matching sounds with appropriate letters; a student with these errors may have difficulty discriminating or segmenting sounds, or 'holding' sounds in short-term auditory memory. He will therefore need visual and lexical strategies for learning.

Column E

Errors in this column may indicate the student is not able to keep track of the whole word, but may 'get lost' in it. The student may have eye-to-hand co-ordination problems, or handwriting problems.

General Comments

If a student has most errors in Column A, it suggests that she is on the way to understanding English spelling convention. The further to the right the errors are, the more difficulty the student is likely to have in acquiring spellings. A large number of errors in Column C may indicate that the student has visual perceptual processing difficulties, with a weak memory for the way words look and problems with making generalisations about language. This is especially likely if they also have errors in Columns A, B and/or E. A student with a large number of errors in Column D is likely to have auditory processing difficulties.

Note: This spelling analysis may not entirely apply to the written work of bilingual students and students with Afro-Caribbean language backgrounds. The way the student perceives the sounds and grammatical features of Standard English may show a need for more tuition in these areas and not any perceptual processing weakness on the part of the student. However, English spelling is not basically phonetic and students need to understand the visual-motor nature of spelling.

Other Points

- If a student omits grammatical endings (e.g. -ed or -s), this is not necessarily because a student doesn't 'hear' them; it may also be that the student hasn't generalised the usage of these endings and may have difficulties with grammatical rules. It is sometimes helpful not to code these sorts of errors until the end, when the student's pattern of difficulties have emerged.

- Short vowel confusions, like *denner* for *dinner*, are not necessarily auditory errors. Often they may signify that the student has difficulty remembering the 'rules' about appropriate letter combinations. Vowel sounds vary so much in English, depending on their context (e.g. 'a' in cat, car, caught, bath, etc), that using them appropriately is often a matter of learning likely letter combinations and having a clear visual image of the word. This is especially true when the vowel is unstressed. Consequently, as a rule of thumb, coding such errors in Column C is less likely to be misleading.

- Students may pronounce words differently according to where they live; for example a London East End student may write 'birfday' for birthday. Such an error does not show a problem with sounds and is an acceptable phonetic rendering if his pronunciation is taken into account; it could therefore be categorised in Column A.

Planning a Spelling Programme

Identifying the patterns of difficulty a student has is important in establishing an appropriate spelling programme.

Usually through a spelling error analysis a student's strategies for attempting spelling will become clear, also their strengths and weaknesses. For example, a student who has most errors in Column C is tending to spell phonetically but is poor in remembering the visual elements of the word, and thus of acquiring a sense of when a word 'looks right'. In addition such a student shows a weakness in generalising from common spelling patterns and rules. This student would need help in learning to use her phonic strengths, by inventing spelling pronunciations to help retrieve the visual image (e.g. par li *a* ment). She would also need help in understanding the structure of words and learning appropriate letter combinations, through word building and word 'families'.

On the other hand, a student with most errors in Column D may be spelling visually but omitting or confusing sounds because he can't 'hear' or retain them. Such a student would benefit from more visual approaches, such as emphasising letter patterns and finding words within words.*

References

Hulley, Jan, *Spelling Dictations*, Loxtrain, Sheffield College, 1922.

Klein, Cynthia and Millar, Robin, *Unscrambling Spelling*, Hodder and Stoughton, 1990.

Klein, Cynthia, *Setting Up a Learning Programme for Adult Dyslexics*, Language and Literacy Unit, 1991.

Peters, Margaret, *Diagnostic and Remedial Spelling Manual*, Macmillan Education, 1975.

* For a full discussion on setting up a spelling programme see Klein and Millar, 1990 and Klein, 1991.

> Late one night my friend ~~wok~~ me saying would yoy enjoy a tryk run in my new helpac I ~~have~~ had scealn sracbe in to my track sunt before ~~wore~~ we were away the lights of the city glow ben to stars above I was beinging to wonder about are desigtion when I caught sight of the spinering knigh eagh of tru surface of what must have been a type of flying sauce wistering round use we dic sillfmlle to anod a accian tence I suddele awoke in the comforley bed I had n acc luf.

An example of a dictation from a student with auditory processing difficulties. Note the visual approach she takes as in *knigh* for *knife*. She generally has a good idea of acceptable letter combinations but can't always relate these appropriately to sound, and in *eagh* for *edge*. She has great difficulty tackling words when she has no visual image for them.

> Lat one night my ~~food~~ friend walke me saying ~~would~~ you engoy a trial run in my new helicopter; had rkearly rkrambled into new trak rait ~~befor~~ we were way the ught of the city glowed henef the stak ~~abou~~ abour. I war ~~begung~~ to oneder about our lerenatio when i cout rit of the re11ng knife edge of the x cirfis of what murt han been a type of flying crear warding around ur me ~~the~~ lodged rkillfully to avoud an ~~ad~~ acident to our relibe the rpace craft regard hight and me rane donier to earth and the comefertcble bed i had never actualy left

An example of dictation from a student with visual-motor processing difficulties. Note that the sounds are usually all there but visual elements are missing or confused and he is not very aware of the 'rules' of English spelling or what 'looks right'. He sometimes takes a lexical approach to spelling as in the creative spelling of *wonder* as *oneder*. Note also the handwriting difficulties, e.g. the 'spidery' quality, the incomplete or awkward construction of some letters and the lack of fluent joining (where the pen has stopped and then started again to look like joining letters). (see appendix for correct version).

Spelling Error Analysis Chart

Date ....

Student's Name ....   Dictation Selection ....Level 2

Script	Error	A	B	C	D	E
late	Cat			✓		
woke	walke					✓
enjoy	enjdy					✓
scarcely	Skeasly				✓	
scrambled	skrambled			✓		
track	trak			✓		
before	befor	✓				
lights	Light				✓ or ✓	
beneath	benet			✓		
stars	star				✓ or ✓	
beginning	begining			✓		
wander	oneder			✓		
destination	dessination				✓	
caught	Caut			✓		
sight	Sit			✓		
spinning	spining			✓		
surface	cirfis			✓		
saucer	cocer			✓		
whistling	wiseling			✓		
skilfully	shillfully			✓		
avoid	avoid			✓ or ✓		
relief	relife		✓			
regained	regand	✓		✓		
neight	hight	✓		✓		
comfortable	comeferteble			✓		
actually	actuaty					✓

A. Logical phonetic alternative and looks like an acceptable English spelling, i.e. follows English spelling convention (e.g. spair/spare; tipe/type; prisition/precision).

B. Visual-sequential (two letters within a word misordered: trail/trial; aviod/avoid) where the confusion is visual rather than sound-based.

C. Shows lack of awareness of spelling rules or acceptable letter combinations (babys for babies; apointed for appointed; pequler for peculiar; glod for glowed).

D. Sounds are misheard or missing or missequenced. (sreet for street; divleved for delivered, cappalled for collapsed, theer for three).

E. Motor: Handwriting/reptition/telescoping, (rember or rememember for remember). Substituting one word for another/ Omitting letters unintentionally.

Observations: Spidery handwriting, picks up pen or stops often between letters, so what look like joining often isn't really. Writes slowly. Seems to have poor visual memory for distinctive letter patterns and takes phonetic approach generally. Sometime uses lexical knowledge as in 'oneder'. Unsure of many vowel combinations. Not keeping track of sentences as in omitting 'my' and omitting plurals — probably concentrating too much on spellings. Oblivious to punctuation

38

Spelling Error Analysis Chart

Date ....

Student's Name .... Dictation Selection ....

Script	Error	A	B	C	D	E

A. Logical phonetic alternative and looks like an acceptable English spelling, i.e. follows English spelling convention (e.g. spair/spare: tipe/type; prisition/precision).
B. Visual-sequential (two letters within a word misordered: trail/trial; aviod/avoid) where the confusion is visual rather than sound-based.
C. Shows lack of awareness of spelling rules or acceptable letter combinations (babys for babies; apointed for appointed; pequler for peculiar; glod for glowed).
D. Sounds are misheard or missing or missequenced. (sreet for street; divleved for delivered, cappalled for collapsed, theer for three).
E. Motor: Handwriting/reptition/telescoping, (rember or rememember for remember). Substituting one word for another/ Omitting letters unintentionally.

Observations:

5 | Writing Analysis

A close analysis of a piece of free writing is an important adjunct to a dictation. Such writing can reveal organisational and expressive language difficulties as well as handwriting difficulties which only occur in a longer written piece, such as letter construction breaking down or frequent 'dropping' of letters and words.

Ask the student to bring a piece of writing, preferably from course work, along to the diagnostic interview. It is useful if the student has not used a dictionary for spellings and if it is a final draft it helps to also see a first draft. Many students have to rewrite course work several times to produce an acceptable draft. It can be of great value to explore the student's experience of and approach to writing as part of the analysis.

The following is a guide to identifying the kinds of difficulties which may contribute to a diagnosis of specific learning difficulties.

However, it is important to view any writing difficulties in the context of the student's experience of writing and in the light of reading, spelling and other difficulties.

Handwriting

- Does the student do joined up writing? Is it regular in formation?

- How does s/he hold the pen? Does s/he press hard? Does s/he have difficulty controlling her/his writing?

- Does s/he confuse *b* and *d* or any other letters, or make any backwards (e.g. 2 for S)?

- Does s/he mix up capital and lower case letters?

- Is the construction of letters awkward or confusing, e.g. open a's (α) or letters which are fused (ω for un)?

- Does s/he frequently drop or add letters unintentionally?

- Is handwriting irregular or variable in size and direction?

Punctuation

- Does s/he use full stops appropriately? Commas?

- Does s/he seem to grasp when a sentence is complete?
  Can s/he make a sentence complete if it is not?

- Does s/he use apostrophes appropriately? Other punctuation?

Syntax

- Does s/he use tense consistently?

- Does s/he use subject-verb agreement consistently?

- Does s/he leave off grammatical endings, e.g. *-ed*?

- Is sentence structure awkward or confusing?

- Does s/he omit words?

- Does s/he use incorrect verb forms (e.g. 'have being' for 'have been')?

- Can s/he restructure sentences?

Vocabulary

- Does s/he use incorrect forms of words (e.g. 'difficultness')?

- Does s/he confuse words with similar constructions (e.g. 'underlying/underlining')?

- Does s/he frequently confuse meanings of words?

Language Difficulties

- Does s/he use roundabout expression to convey ideas?

- Does s/he use repetitive phrasing or words?

- Does s/he use simplified language to convey complex thoughts?

- Does s/he have problems finding the 'right' words or the 'right' way to say something?

- Is written expression generally confused (i.e. the ideas are 'there' but not clearly expressed)?

Organisation

- Does s/he have problems sequencing or putting ideas in order?

- Can s/he make and follow a plan?

- Can s/he:
  - keep to the point?
  - select main ideas?
  - expand an idea?
  - group ideas/categorise?

General

- Does s/he write drafts/edit own work?

- Does s/he use paragraphing appropriately?

- Does s/he proof-read own work?
  - can s/he find errors?
  - can s/he correct errors?

- Can s/he understand and apply conventions of formal written English (e.g. introduction and conclusion, use of transitional phrases)?

An example of a piece of a psychology student's essay:

Schizophreina is the lable appied to a group of disorders, charcterized by servere personality disorganizhon, distortion of realty and an inability ro funchon in daily life.
Most experts belife. Schizophreina encompasses several disorders. Each of which may have a diffrent cause.
Schinozophrinia is the historical term, and one still most commonly used.

It accures in all cultures, even those that are remote from the stress of Modern Civilization It appears to have plauged humanity throughout History.

Schizophreinia Usally appears in young adulthood, the peak ages are between 25-35. Experts are now looking back at these age groups. There is belifs that it may even start from birth "The schizophrenic child BY Dr Sheila Canton".

Somhimes the disorders develop slowly as a gradual process of Increasing Seclusivness, and inapropriate behaviour. Somtimes it appears sudden, marked by intense confusion. Wheather the disorde develops slowly or Suddenly, the sympror are many and varied.

Schizophrenic individuals Usally fail to exsibit

A summary of a writing analysis of this student would note the lack of joined up writing and the unevenness and large size and somewhat immature appearance of the writing. The spelling is erratic, e.g. schizophrenia is spelled several different ways throughout. Spelling errors indicate poor visual memory and some motor integration difficulties expressed through telescoping, as in *charcterized* and *disorganiztion*. The writing seems very abbreviated; she probably needs help with understanding the form and conventions of an essay, and she is not completely clear about paragraphing. She knows she's supposed to give references, but doesn't know how to do it. Her points are direct and appropriate but she needs to learn how to expand them, organize them into larger units and give examples. She is very unclear about the use of punctuation and grammar is hazy, as in 'There is belifs' and 'sudden' rather than 'suddenly'. She appears to need help with editing and proofreading to 'see' her errors. Expressive language seems generally good but where she has written 'Experts are now looking back at these age groups', she seems to actually mean that they are looking beyond these age groups at younger ones or that they are revising this view; she may therefore need help to develop more exact written expression.

6 | Drawing Conclusions

Anything which becomes clear at the interview can be shared with the student at that time; often the student's comments will help to illuminate her difficulties. The whole process, ideally, is tutor and student looking together at the evidence accumulating in front of them. However, it is usually necessary to reflect at some length on the evidence to determine whether the student is dyslexic and what sort of language processing problems are dominant.

At this stage, try to pull together all the information that has been collected and look at each aspect of the diagnosis in the light of all the others. Are there factors from the interview and reading, writing and spelling analyses which suggest visual processing difficulties, visual confusions, a weak visual memory? Are there factors which suggest auditory processing problems, weak discrimination and blending skills, poor auditory memory? Are there factors which suggest poor motor integration, motor tracking? Are there patterns of difficulties with memorising, sequencing, direction, word retrieval? Are the difficulties specific, persistent and intractable in spite of the student's efforts and perhaps extra help at school? Do other factors such as second language interference, missing a lot of school, etc., seem to account for the difficulties or do these seem inadequate to explain them? Are there significant discrepancies between the student's oral and written abilities, and/or between her reading and spelling level?

Often, from a complete diagnosis, the tutor can determine both whether the student is dyslexic and whether the specific difficulties are primarily auditory or visual and if there is a significant motor component. However, sometimes it is necessary to work with the student over a period of time to observe the student's *learning style:* is the student a 'quick forgetter', does she have difficulties generalising, applying 'rules', remembering names or facts as well as spellings, 'seeing' errors, coping with sequence and order? Do the difficulties persist in spite of appropriate tuition?

It is useful to remember that diagnosis is an art rather than a science; it is seeing how the various factors of a student's difficulties form a learning *pattern* and what this reveals about a learner's strengths and weaknesses.

7 | Overview of Specific Learning Difficulties

The following are some general observations about characteristics that seem to go together. Not all are always true for students who manifest these difficulties.

Visual Processing Problems

Background

Look for incidence of squint or amblyopia as a youngster (7-10).

Reading

1. Students may not have been aware of difficulties until junior school.

2. *Advanced readers:* Jerky style. Visual tracking problems evident. Phonetic attack usually fairly adequate. Sometimes they are aware they are 'poor' or 'slow' readers. Often misread familiar words.

3. *Other levels:* May read upside down with better comprehension. Have difficulties recognising words.

4. *Comprehension:* Student may need to re-read passage several times to remember significant details. Spontaneous recall is vague.

5. *General:* Distracted by typographical errors, may not use punctuation cues, does not often correct errors or monitor comprehension. Sometimes print 'jumps' or 'blurs'.

Spelling

1. Errors are, in the majority, phonetic alternatives, but often fail to follow English spelling convention.

2. Rule based errors are common (partys for parties).

3. Visual sequencing errors may be common (naer for near).

Handwriting

Handwriting may not be disordered although b/d confusion may continue to exist in advanced writers; however, visual-motor difficulties often go together.

Other

Easily distracted visually. General directional confusions common. Difficulty seeing errors.

Auditory Processing Problems

Background

Look for evidence of ear infections; severe bouts of bronchitis or tonsilitis; glue ear, etc (ages 3-8); minor speech difficulties; 'late talkers'.

Reading

1. Severe reading difficulties as children.

2. *Advanced readers:* Major problems in decoding unfamiliar words. Other than this can be quite fluent readers. Often have good comprehension.

3. *Other readers:* Same as above, but many more errors; may need additional reading strategies.

4. *General:* Rely heavily on context.

Spelling

1. Often use visual approach. Phonetic approach generally unsuccessful.

2. Spellings are very disordered. Major sounds may be missing, especially l/r blends; medial m/n unaccented syllables.

3. Sequencing errors involving sound confusions are common (gril for girl, fuirt for fruit).

4. Spellings are very difficult to acquire.

5. Syllables may be omitted or missequenced (imediale for immediately, capalled for collapsed).

Handwriting

No significant problems.

Other

May be distracted auditorally.

Motor Processing Problems

Background

Look for co-ordination difficulties as youngsters (especially eye/hand); articulation difficulties; handwriting problems.

Reading

1. May not have significant difficulties in reading, but may have problems crossing midline so need to put text to one side to read.
2. Visual tracking may be a problem.

Spelling

1. Many spellings phonetically accurate.
2. Spelling errors usually include:
   – omission of syllables
   – repetition of syllables or letters
   – unintentional omission or addition of letters.

Handwriting

1. Handwriting difficulties may be severe.
2. Constructional and directional problems may be evident.
3. Other indications:
   – lack of connected writing
   – scratchy or variable style
   – irregular formation or poor construction of letters
   – inability to stay on the line
   – irregular size of letters.
4. May not be able to write fast enough to complete work or letter construction may break down.
5. May have to press hard to control writing.

Other

- May not have attentional difficulties of those with auditory or visual problems.

- Planning and organising difficulties; especially with essays, assignments, discursive writing.

Persistent Learning Difficulties for most Dyslexic Students

- Memorising names, facts.

- Remembering sequences (e.g. alphabet, instructions).

- Rote memory tasks in maths
  1) times tables
  2) basic number facts.

- Right/left discrimination.

- Learned to tell time late, may still have problems.

- Concentration difficulties or easily distracted.

- Severe expressive writing problems even when orally competent.

- Copying difficulties.

- Word retrieval – getting ideas down on paper.

8 | Writing Reports and Making Recommendations

The Diagnostic Report

It is useful to write a diagnostic report for several reasons: it allows us as tutors to identify, clarify and summarise the student's difficulties for ourselves and the student, and to make recommendations for supporting the student in the classroom, in examinations and in individual tuition.

When writing a report we need to consider *why* we are writing it (e.g. to get examination provision, to recommend learning support, to obtain support for the student from other tutors, to help the student understand her difficulties) and *who* we are writing it for (e.g. the student, tutors, employers, examining boards). The report should be written in accordance with our aims. A report for examination provision, for example, needs to be fairly concise but clearly make the case for the kinds of difficulties the student experiences in reading, writing and spelling, the persistent and specific nature of these difficulties in spite of appropriate tuition and how they are exacerbated under examination conditions.

When writing for other tutors, the aim is to help them to see how students' difficulties will affect them in the classroom, in their specific subject areas, and how they can be helped. It is important that other tutors understand the kind of difficulties students have so they will not be misperceived as lazy, careless or incompetent.

It is also important to be sensitive to the student's feelings about the report, to go through the report with the student and be willing to change wording until the report is acceptable to the student. Only those personal details which are necessary should be included and these should be put as generally as possible. For instance, one student was upset by the comment that his mother also had these difficulties as he felt she was being 'blamed'. Changing the wording to 'other members of his family have similar difficulties' resolved the problem.

Recommendations

Examination boards and higher education institutions make various provision in written examinations for students with specific learning difficulties. GCSE and 'A' Level boards will generally grant extra time and/or sympathetic consideration for spelling and writing difficulties. Other provision may be granted by different examining bodies or higher education institutions, e.g. a separate room, an amanuensis, a reader, use of a word processor or an oral examination. The student should be consulted about what provision she would like and it may be useful to talk through the options.

Recommendations for developing written language skills might include recommendations that the student should:

(i)   Follow a course of study making regular reading and writing demands (if not already doing this). Students should be encouraged to use the words they want in their writing rather than stay confined by the words they can spell.

(ii)   Receive regular 1:1 learning support to work on their specific language and learning needs. Dyslexic students often have great difficulty applying conventions and procedures and need support in practising them in their own writing. They usually need help with essay planning and organising, editing and proofreading. Assessment of priority needs should be updated from new writing each week.

(iii)   Follow an individually structured spelling programme*. Most dyslexic students need to learn spellings; a spelling programme provides a core of the support work which reveals more clearly to student and teacher the student's particular learning style and needs, and can demonstrate constantly why a student needs to learn in a particular way.

    The spelling programme gives immediate rewards if done properly; the multisensory learning and systematic revision works for most students, particularly if the strategies for remembering are tailored to their perceptual strengths.

(iv)   Work on devising strategies for improving reading. The spelling programme can often help with reading; the visual chunking gives an alternative approach to someone who can't sound out, and it can also help build word recognition. However, students may also need to develop comprehension techniques for reading. In addition, for some students, a sheet of coloured (often pink, yellow or blue) acetate placed over a page can reduce glare or figure/ground 'jumping' and a card under the line being read can aid visual tracking.

A student may have other immediate needs revealed by the interview for which a recommendation may be helpful. For instance, quiet provision was recommended once for a YTS Trainee who had to work where loud music was played and who had severe auditory difficulties.

---

* Such a programme is outlined in *Unscrambling Spelling* by Cynthia Klein and Robin Millar.

The learning support tutor may need to liaise or help the student liaise with subject staff by making appropriate recommendations; for instance, giving students copies of a tutor's notes rather than expecting them to take dictation or developing proofreading skills through error analysis marking of students' written work.

Great care should be given to making recommendations as they offer a basis and structure for supporting the student and an opportunity to ensure a programme and network of support which can enable the student to succeed and reach her potential.

Example of a diagnostic report by a Learning Support tutor in a Further Education College

---

Re: S

'S' was referred to me for a diagnosis of her specific learning difficulties. She is currently studying A-Level Film Studies and Art History and also GCSE Maths to improve her grade.

Her tutors report a very great discrepancy between her oral performance and the level of her written work.

Background

'S' has always had difficulty with her reading and writing and received extra help in junior and secondary schools. Until the age of 7 or 8 she did mirror writing. She was late learning to tell the time and still finds this difficult, she also has left/right confusions. Learning the alphabet and the times tables was a problem for her and the latter persists to some extent. Asked to say the months of the year backwards, she could manage this but very slowly showing the continuation of a sequencing difficulty. 'S' sometimes has difficulty pronouncing multisyllabic words, e.g. 'monopoly' and 'jewellery' and experienced some fine motor coordination problems as a child. Other members of 'S''s family have had similar difficulties.

Reading

'S' read a post-GCSE text for assessment. In spite of a large number of errors, she read fairly fluently, repeating and correcting words to make sense and making good use of punctuation. She made guesses at unknown words substituting visually similar words, e.g. 'valued' for 'valid' and 'research' for 'reaction' and trying to make sense in the context. When she could not guess a word she used a phonetic attack which often let her down; sometimes a word was omitted after a try at the first syllable. Several times in trying to decode she misread b for d. There was some omission and insertion of small words. This was sometimes to create a familiar phrase in context, e.g. 'they have to be asked' for 'than to ask'. However when 'S' omitted the word 'not' it totally changed the meaning of the sentence.

'S' 's comprehension was quite good overall including drawing inferences but was generally not so good on detail due to her misreading.

Spelling

'S' has severe spelling difficulties making some of her work very difficult to read. Given a dictation for assessment, her errors were mostly due to a sound or syllable being misheard or omitted, e.g. 'souteren' for 'southern' and 'enthogesten' for 'enthusiasm', the substitute often being visually similar to the original word. There is also some indication here that 'S' has difficulty holding the sound of the word and sometimes omits or confuses syllables, e.g. 'destreced' for 'distinguished'.

'S' described how when writing her 'hand takes over and extra letters creep in'. This motor integration problem can be seen with extra letters in e.g. 'conduition' for 'condition', with telescoping in e.g. 'delived' for 'delivered' and 'altube' for 'altitude' (note b for d), and with word replacement in '*rangen*' for 'region' (following mountainous).

A few errors indicate that like many people with specific learning difficulties 'S' may not have internalised some common spelling rules, e.g. 'frezzing' for 'freezing' and 'requsting' for 'requesting'. 'S' was able to identify about a third of her mistakes when proofreading and never identified a correct word as being incorrect.

The same pattern of spelling errors appears in 'S's' essay writing.

Writing

'S's' handwriting is cursive and, although variable in style, shows there is the basis for a well-formed clear script. There is some poor construction of letters, a device which is often developed to disguise poor spelling. However, this could be a further indication of her motor coordination difficulty, as is the fusion observed in words such as 'do*wn*' and 'instrumen*ts*' where the underlined letters appear fused together.

When 'S' is writing essays or assignments her difficulties with spelling interfere with the way she expresses herself. She says she has 'to use different words and this is less expressive'. This also slows down the flows of her writing and affects her punctuation and the structure of her work.

Under pressure of examinations these difficulties will be much more pronounced and some of her work is likely to become unreadable.

Diagnosis and Recommendations

'S' appears to have specific learning difficulties (dyslexia) of an auditory perceptual nature, exacerbated by motor integration problems.

1. In the past, 'S' has been allowed 25% extra time for her GCSE exams. Because of the persistent nature of her difficulties, including her recent misreading of a mock exam question and the illegibility of some of her writing, examination boards are now being asked to award her the following:

(a) Access to a reader who can read both the rubric and the questions.

(b) Use of an amanuensis to give her full use of the expressive language evident in her oral work.

(c) In the event of an amanuensis being disallowed, 'S' to be able to write the exam and then read it into a tape recorder.

(d) Extra time (15 minutes per hour of examination) for any written examination.

(e) Sympathetic consideration of her spelling difficulties in any written work at grade awarding level.

2. I would recommend that all 'S's tutors be made aware that 'S's errors are not due to carelessness or lack of effort but to her specific learning difficulties. She needs considerably more time for completing her work because of the extra time she needs for reading, planning, rewriting and proofreading her work.

'S' says she has difficulty with note-taking in her classes and these are the notes she will use for revision. The provision of handouts could be helpful here or 'S' might want to consider asking another student or the lecturer if she can photocopy her notes.

3. Some students with specific learning difficulties find use of a word-processor of considerable help. Apart from allowing them to correct, revise and re-order work, it can help improve the spelling particularly where there are motor coordination difficulties. 'S' might wish to explore the idea of using a word-processor at the college. It would be helpful for her to develop keyboard skills.

4. 'S' would benefit from some individual learning support. This should include an individual spelling programme using the Look, Cover, Write, Check method in the way described in 'Unscrambling Spelling'. A visual approach would seem appropriate and would help 'S's reading and proofreading, in addition to her spelling. Handwriting could be worked on at the same time. I would be pleased to offer 'S' this support at the college.

Learning Support Tutor, Specific Learning Difficulties

9 | Telling a Student About Dyslexia

After having a diagnostic session, many students want to know more about the how and why of their condition. Dyslexia is a disability or specific learning difficulty which needs to be identified and clarified with the student. This is not because of some desire to label students, but because students need to understand that their difficulties will not go away with tuition, practice, hard work, etc. If the student is an adult with severe spelling difficulties, that student will always have spelling difficulties. Students deserve to be told what we understand to be their difficulties, the hardships these may impose on them, and the support they are entitled to. They also need to be assured that they *can* learn and improve, and succeed in spite of these difficulties.

Some students are shocked to discover the extent of their difficulties and need many hours of support and guidance to come to terms with what dyslexia means to them. On the other hand, a substantial number of students are relieved to have their difficulties acknowledged and explained, to find that others have the same kinds of difficulties they have and that educators are concerned about improving tuition for dyslexic students.

Tutors should not begin to assume that the student is dyslexic until *a complete diagnosis* is in hand. Too many factors can influence the reasons an adult student is not learning and these must be fully explored in order to make a reliable estimation of the kind of difficulties the student might have. Some students are not interested in exploring their disability further and the diagnosis and teaching or examination recommendations may be enough for these students.

The tutor should discuss the diagnosis *in detail* before moving on to a discussion of dyslexia.

Explaining the Diagnosis

In discussing the diagnosis, many points will have come up during the diagnostic interview. Students will often begin to make connections about their different difficulties during the interview and this should be encouraged. For instance, one student began to see how her difficulties in copying were related to other difficulties; another, how mistakes in telling the time were part of the dyslexic pattern.

It is useful in discussing the diagnosis to help students understand their strengths and weaknesses as a way of laying the basis for setting up a learning programme. In talking through the reading analysis it is helpful to show a student, for example, that her difficulty with comprehension is because she tries too much to work out the look and sound of a word without paying enough attention to meaning and grammatical structure. This can be done by using Venn diagrams (see Helen Arnold, 1982), or some other method to show the student the kinds of miscues she made and explain what these mean. You might want to show another student how he is using meaning and syntax to predict because he can't seem to decode the words; this may be a good way into talking about his difficulty in discriminating sounds or translating letters into sounds.

A similar approach can be taken with spelling. Students often find it very revealing and reassuring to categorise their own errors*; they then realise that they make certain *types* of mistakes and that there is a 'method' in their approach to spelling.

Students also benefit from understanding that their organisational, planning and sequencing difficulties are part of the pattern of difficulties and not just a result of laziness or carelessness on their part. To discover that getting lost, being late or disorganised may also be connected to their reading and spelling difficulties can also help release a sense of guilt and failure and enable a new confidence.

It is also important to go through a written report with a student because seeing their difficulties spelled out in print can be distressing even though these have been previously acknowledged.

Explaining Dyslexia

For students who want to know more about dyslexia there are a number of approaches which can offer a jumping off point from which to explore the subtle nature of specific learning difficulties. These approaches are by no means the only way to discuss dyslexia (students among themselves are often better at it), but offer possible guidelines for a tutor to begin.

1. The Brain (see diagram)

This drawing of the brain has purposefully been made very simple so that you can draw on it as appropriate. One way of using it is the following:

(a) If the student appears to have auditory perceptual problems, indicate how auditory information is processed.

1. Information goes into the ears OK. (Student can hear).
2. Indicate which area of the brain processes certain auditory information: e.g. left-language, right-music, environmental sounds, etc.
3. Show how some messages are sent directly to the language centre (ipsi-lateral) but most are sent over the corpus callosum to the other side (contra-lateral) and this is the main route.
4. Explain that there is a problem in the processing or retrieval of auditory information having to do with language.

* A discussion on this along with a form for students to use can be found in Klein & Millar, 1990.

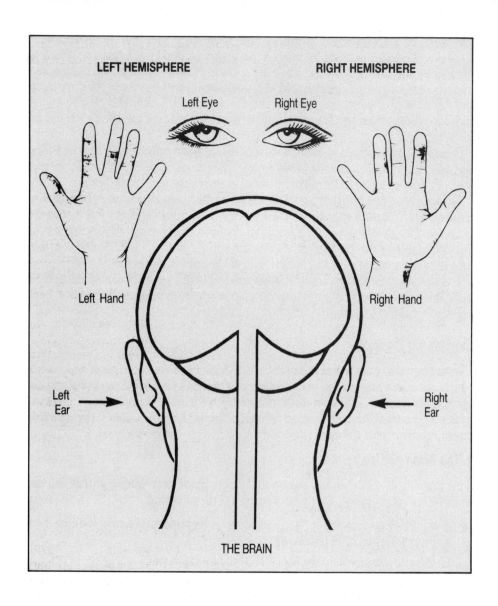

LEFT HEMISPHERE   RIGHT HEMISPHERE

Left Eye   Right Eye

Left Hand   Right Hand

Left Ear   Right Ear

THE BRAIN

(b) If the student appears to have visual processing difficulties, use the same process as (a) except via the eyes; explain that the student may have problems retrieving a visual sequence or recognising words in print.

(c) If the student appears to have motor control problems the problem area is in the motor strip on each side of the corpus callosum.

(d) If several areas seem affected, e.g. visual-motor, then explain how information is processed from one area of the brain to another, and how eye-hand coordination can be affected.

The more severe the dyslexic difficulties, the more areas are probably involved. Usually several areas are likely to be affected.

It should be emphasized here that students need to understand that we are not discussing their intellectual potential but rather specific aspects in processing linguistic information. It can be helpful to say that the student has misfiled information and specialised tuition helps file it correctly. It is also helpful to discuss specific problems such as how a student can miscopy and not identify errors when she doesn't have a good visual sense, or why a student can spell when she knows what the words look like but can't even guess when she doesn't because she can't 'sound out'.

It is especially useful here to talk about the way the brain is organised, that for most people the left brain has developed to specialise in speech and language functions. This left side of the brain works in an analytical, sequential way. The right side of the brain specialises in visual-spatial thinking and functions in a holistic way. Some studies indicate that the dyslexic brain may be more symmetrical and less specialised for language. It may be that language is processed on both sides of the brain, so causing more confusion in processing or at least less specialisation in these language functions Current research suggests that many dyslexic people are more right-brained, holistic thinkers and this puts them at a disadvantage in a culture where written language is given the highest priority and status. It is useful here to relate this to the student's own particular strengths and weaknesses. It can be helpful to use the analogy of the face – what comes first? The eyes? The mouth? The chin? The difficulties of putting a face into a sequence are similar to those the dyslexic person experiences in trying to organise language.

2. Written Language Processing

Some languages (Chinese for example) are analogic, that is they use pictographs that visually indicate what the word means (e.g. 人 looks a bit like a man). In English the word 'man' does not look like a man at all but is rather a collection of three arbitrary symbols to represent the sounds we make when we say 'man'. These symbols, m-a-n, are arbitrary and have no particular meaning in relation to the word 'man'; they are therefore more difficult to learn and must be learned by memorising. Memorising arbitrary symbols as in m-a-n rely on the 'working memory' to store and retrieve (or 'file') them as contrasted to long-term memory which is based on meaning and association of ideas or images. Dyslexic people have difficulties with memorising but can learn well when an activity has meaning and they can make meaningful connections. This is why they need different strategies to learn.

It is useful at this point to bring in the student's school experience, e.g. the difficulties in diagnosing children, why she didn't get appropriate help in school, how some children develop late, etc.

3. Analogy with Electricity

A comparison can be made between electricity and nerve impulses. In specific areas of the brain the nerve impulses are not effectively working. This is why it seems that the student can remember certain words at times and forget them at others. In other words, there is a 'short' occasionally in the connections that these nerve impulses make. When one considers that millions of nerve connections need to be made for each thinking or doing activity, it is not surprising that confusions and forgetting occur for a student who is not efficiently processing information. Some researchers believe the nerves may have a minor chemical imbalance or some minor damage to the myelin sheath and this causes these irregular connections.

These are three of the most meaningful interpretations of the technical side of dyslexia to use with students. Each of these approaches needs far more development with students – these are only guidelines. Students may wish to know more about their disability. Discussions about what dyslexia is may become an ongoing part of learning support, helping students to make sense of their difficulties and why and how specialist tuition and particular strategies can help. It is very important to communicate to students that their difficulties have *meaning* and can be understood, and that they *can* learn.

References

Arnold, Helen, *Listening to Children Read*, Hodder & Stoughton, 1982.

Klein, Cynthia and Millar, Robin, *Unscrambling Spelling*, Hodder & Stoughton, 1990.

Springer, Sally and Deutch, Georg, *Left Brain, Right Brain*, W.H. Freeman and Co., 1981.

Appendix I

The Reading Process

'Reading is a matter of extracting, relating and processing cues to decode a precise message.' (Marie Clay)

In order to diagnose a student's difficulties in reading and to identify strengths and weaknesses in reading it is necessary to be clear about how efficient readers read, how reading strategies develop in learners and how language processing difficulties may affect readers.

Defining and describing the reading process has not been an easy task and a number of conflicting theories have arisen in the attempt, all emphasising different aspects of the process and based on a variety of models and research in different areas.

Frank Smith, Kenneth Goodman and others from a background of psycholinguistics have described the reading process as a 'psycholinguistic guessing game' which 'involves an interaction between thought and language' (K. Goodman, 1967). They claimed that the fluent reader uses a minimum of clues from written material to arrive at meaning, 'sampling' a piece of writing on the basis of the knowledge they bring to it, and confirming and predicting from their knowledge of linguistic structures and meaning. Goodman wrote, 'Efficient reading does not result from precise perception and identification of all elements, but from a skill in selecting the fewest most productive cues necessary to produce guesses which are right first time. The ability to anticipate that which has not been seen, of course, is vital in reading, just as the ability to anticipate what has not yet been heard is vital in listening' (K. Goodman 1967). It followed from this model that the beginning reader or the poor reader would rely more heavily on *graphic* cues and that the fluent and experienced reader would rely more on *prediction* from context and less on graphic cues.

Although few people would disagree that reading is an interactive process, more recent research has suggested that fluent processing of written language relies on rapid word recognition rather than context, and that it is the *poor reader* who needs to rely more heavily on context. 'Recent evidence and argument goes against the long-held opinion that context aids word recognition and suggests instead that skilled readers are content to use rapid, efficient stimulus-driven processes to extract meaning from print' (Ellis, 1984).

Research in cognitive psychology suggests that efficient readers have an *internal lexicon* which they access by rapid and automatic sight recognition. They use context to construct meaning from words as they read, compensate for slow or incomplete lexical access to difficult words, to select from alternative word meanings and to detect errors. However, this is very different from using context to *predict*, which is actually a rather slow and unnecessarily laborious method of reading, and not always successful. This can be shown by the passage below, where Polish words have been inserted throughout the text to simulate words the reader does not recognise and cannot 'decode', so that the reader must rely on context for working out words.

Czytanie, jak thinking, is a zkomplikowany process. When ty myślisz, all you have to do jest to produkować the responses from within you. Kiedy you read you have to produce responses które są precisely the ones the author pisał. You have to match twoje mysli do autora.

It is worth remembering that even if we *can* read by using context and minimal visual cues, that is not necessarily the way we *do* read. The disadvantage of reading like this should be apparent to anyone who has tried to read a photocopied piece of writing where some words were smudged or faint, or some letters missing at the end or beginning of each line.

The Developmental Perspective

The *learner* reader, however, does need to use context on the way to becoming a proficient reader. It is also important to note that children learning to read will pass through stages where they use different strategies. The *'emergent'* or **pre-reading** stage, according to Linnea Ehri, is when children learn about print and reading and 'learn the shapes and sounds of most alphabet letters . . . and acquire rudimentary awareness of sounds in words.'

The **first** stage of reading is the *initial reading or decoding* stage when they learn 'how the spelling system represents spoken language', ie the letter-sound system. The two predictors of success at this stage are letter-name knowledge and phonemic segmentation skill. Even at this stage, the better readers look at letters to guess words rather than guess using context.

In the **second** stage, the *fluency* stage, children become faster at decoding unfamiliar words, read known words more easily and faster, and integrate word reading with text comprehension processes. They develop the ability to 'read sight words as rapidly as they can name single letters or digits, indicating that sight words are being processed as single units rather than letter by letter.'

In the **third** stage, the *reading to learn* stage, they can read well enough 'to comprehend more difficult material whose ideas are unfamiliar.' Also at this stage, 'intelligence is more highly correlated with reading skill ... and the amount of reading that students do becomes a major determiner of differences that distinguish good from poor readers.'

Research shows that 'students who have difficulty learning to read are almost always deficient in their knowledge about the spelling system and in their ability to read sight words effectively' (Ehri 1991).

The Two Routes to Reading

Uta Frith's model of the acquisition of literacy suggest three stages, which may overlap: The *logographic* stage, where words are identified by distinguishing visual features; the *alphabetic* stage, based on phoneme awareness where the letter-sound system is mastered; the *orthographic* stage which is based on visual analysis and is independent of sound (Snowling, 1985).

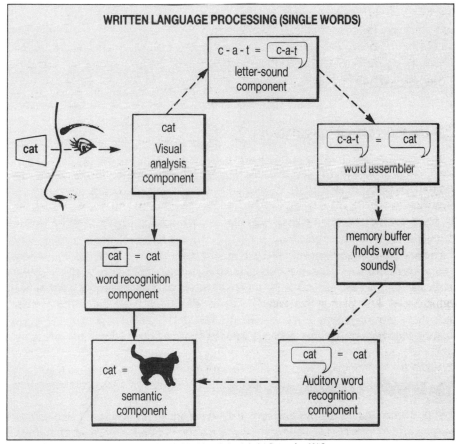

Adapted from 'How the Brain Copes with Words', 'New Scientist', 26 September 1985.

Researchers have identified two routes of reading, which have been shown to operate independently; these are the *phonological* and the *visual* routes. The phonological or 'mediated' route corresponds to Frith's alphabetic stage: the reader 'sounds out' the word. The visual or 'immediate' route corresponds to her orthographic stage. The diagram on the previous page shows a simplified model of the reading of single words. It is easy to see that the visual route (from word recognition to meaning) is more direct.

Using Frith's model it is possible to hypothesize that a reader may 'get stuck' at the alphabetic stage and never become skilled in word recognition. Such a reader may need to rely on 'sounding out', a slower and less satisfactory route which also impedes comprehension because the reader's attention is concentrated on the complex process of working out the words rather than constructing and monitoring meaning.

The following is an attempt to show what it is like to read by sounding out rather than recognising words:

Wreeding in thiss weigh menes yoo mussed konsentrait on sownding out eech werd sow itt wood bee difecult too komprehende a longue passudge.

It is also possible to identify the reader who fails to master the alphabetic stage, and in spite of 'leapfrogging' to the orthographic stage, is never able to use the phonological route when faced with unfamiliar words or as a monitoring device. Because the letter-sound system is never mastered, knowledge about the spelling system is weak and cannot be used effectively to aid word recognition.

Some researchers refer to these two types of readers as the 'Phoenician' and the 'Chinese' readers. The 'Phoenician' reader relies 'more heavily than the average reader on phonic mediation,' whereas the 'Chinese' reader 'relies heavily on whole-word visual identification.' However, 'extreme Chinese and Phoenician readers are rare animals. The normal pattern is for a person to be good, mediocre or poor at both whole-word and phonic processing.' When looking at dyslexic reading styles, however, 'we are looking at *relative* not absolute development of differential whole-word and phonic recognition skills.' (Ellis, 1984).

The Interactive-Compensatory Model

Frank Smith and Kenneth Goodman may be seen as proposing a 'top-down' or *language based* view of reading, suggesting that readers look for meaning first, 'rather than strive to identify letters or words' (F Smith. 1978). Thus readers would start at the 'top' or higher level of *meaning* and work 'down' to the lower levels of *words* and *letters*. They proposed this view in response to the 'bottom up' view that *decoding* is central to reading development. This view proposes that readers analyse what they read initially at the level of visual features, then letter patterns corresponding to sound units and finally word perception, working up to meaning last. Although the 'bottom-up' view does not take into account readers' knowledge about language, research has shown that the 'top-down' or language-based view does not give an accurate picture of the skilled reader's use of rapid word recognition, and that it is inefficient to read by prediction.

More recently, Stanovitch (1980) and others have proposed an *interactive-compensatory* model, whereby both 'bottom-up' and 'top-down' processes are going on simultaneously. According to the interactive view, information from the printed page is processed 'bottom-up' starting from letters, then words, clause meanings and so on. However, the reader also has expectations which act 'top-down' toward lower levels. 'The essence of the interactive view is that high-level processes constrain low-level ones. Stanovitch has pointed out an interesting implication of the interactive view; namely, that normal processes at one level can compensate for deficient processes at another level. For example, if somebody were poor at the low-level skill of word identification, they would rely more heavily on high-level factors such as sentence context' (Jorm 1983).

Stanovitch argues that children *do* 'use context in a compensatory manner so that when decoding skill is poor, and therefore proceeds slowly, context facilitates processing. When decoding becomes automatic and therefore proceeds rapidly, context has no effect' (Snowling, 1987).

Jorm comments that the finding that poor readers 'make greater use of context to aid word identification is surprising because . . . they are generally poorer at comprehension as well as word identification . . . They are often poorer at predicting a missing word on the basis of the preceding context . . . However, there is a crucial difference between *being able* to predict from context and actually *making use* of this capability. Although normal readers can make better predictions from context, they make less use of this skill in word identification. The reason that normal readers rely less on context is that they do not have the same need for it because they can identify words quite well on the basis of their visual features' (Jorm). The fluent reader uses context primarily for error detection and monitoring meaning. 'The fluent reader needs to know if the text being read makes sense and matches expectation; and if it does not meet these criteria, whether the fault lies with the author, the mechanism of transmission (e.g. a misprint) or the reader . . .' (Philip T Smith).

'The compensatory hypothesis is important not only because it gives a description of the reading strategies used by (poor) readers, but also because . . . it may be possible to help (them) to rely more heavily on those components of the reading process in which they are not deficient' (Jorm).

This means that the student with weak word recognition or decoding skills may need to be encouraged to make better use of context to predict and monitor their reading. The interactive-compensatory model is thus a useful one not only for understanding the reading process, but also for suggesting strategies to help poor readers compensate for their weaknesses.

References

Kenneth Goodman, 'Reading: A Psycholinguistic Guessing Game', *Journal of the Reading Specialist*, May 1967.

Andrew Ellis, *Reading, Writing and Dyslexia*, Lawrence Erlbaum Associates, 1984.

Philip T. Smith, 'The Development of Reading: the Acquisition of a Cognitive Skill' in *Language Acquisition*, eds Paul Fletcher and Michael Garman, Cambridge University Press, 1986.

Linnea Ehri, 'The Development of Reading and Spelling in Children: an Overview', in *Dyslexia: Integrating Theory and Practice*, eds M Snowling and M Thomson, Whurr, 1991.

Margaret Snowling, 'The Assessment of Reading and Spelling Skills' in *Children's Written Language Difficulties*, ed M Snowling, NFER-Nelson, 1985.

Margaret Snowling, *Dyslexia: A Cognitive Developmental Perspective*, Basil Blackwell, 1987.

Frank Smith, *Understanding Reading*, Holt, Rinehart and Winston, 1978.

A.F. Jorm, *The Psychology of Reading and Spelling Difficulties*, Routledge and Kegan Paul, 1983.

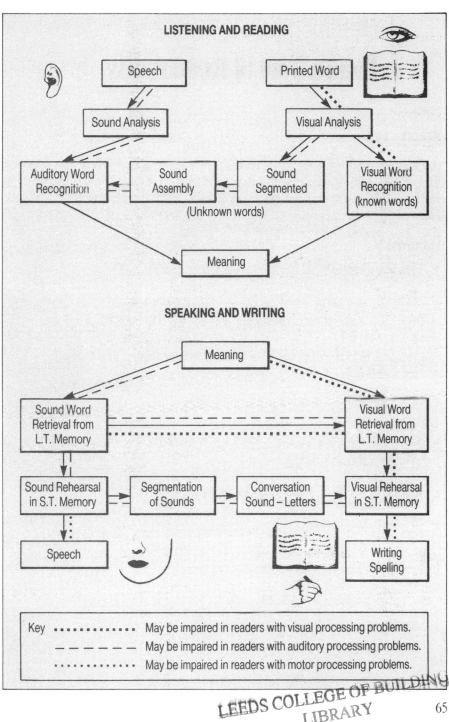

LISTENING AND READING

Speech → Sound Analysis

Printed Word → Visual Analysis

Auditory Word Recognition ← Sound Assembly ← Sound Segmented

Visual Word Recognition (known words)

(Unknown words)

Meaning

SPEAKING AND WRITING

Meaning

Sound Word Retrieval from L.T. Memory → Visual Word Retrieval from L.T. Memory

Sound Rehearsal in S.T. Memory → Segmentation of Sounds → Conversation Sound – Letters → Visual Rehearsal in S.T. Memory

Speech

Writing Spelling

Key .... May be impaired in readers with visual processing problems.
     – – – – – – May be impaired in readers with auditory processing problems.
     .... May be impaired in readers with motor processing problems.

Fogg's Test of Readability

Introduction

A quick and convenient method of checking levels of reading difficulty of any material with 100+ words giving reading age equivalents. It tends, however, to give high results so this should be taken into account when determining the level of a text.

Procedure

1. Take any sample of 100 words in complete sentences.

2. Count the number of sentences by counting the full stops; if the last full sentence stops short of the 100th word, count only the full sentences for this stage.

3. Count the number of words with three or more syllables. Omit capitalised words such as names.

4. Divide the number of sentences into 100; answer = x.

5. Add the number of words with more than three syllables to your answer, ie x + y; y being the number of words.

6. Multiply x + y by 0.3 to give an American grade equivalent.

7. Add 5.0 to your answer to give the equivalent to an English reading age.

8. Example = four complete sentences and nine words with three or more syllables.

   a) 4. $\dfrac{100}{25}$ b) $25 + 9 = 34$ c) $\begin{array}{r} 34 \\ \underline{0.3} \\ \underline{10.2} \end{array}$ d) $10.2 + 5 = 15.2$

The material has a reading age of c. 15 years.

Reading Age Level of Materials Based on Fogg Index
Sample size = 100 words

Number of Sentences (N)

	4	6	8	10	12	14	16	18	20	22	24	26	28	30	32	34
0	12.5	10.0	8.8	8.0	7.5	7.1	6.9	6.7	6.5	6.4	6.3	6.2	6.1	6.0	5.9	5.9
1	12.8	10.3	9.1	8.3	7.8	7.4	7.2	7.0	6.8	6.7	6.6	6.5	6.4	6.3	6.2	6.2
2	13.1	10.6	9.4	8.6	8.1	7.7	7.5	7.3	7.1	7.0	6.9	6.8	6.7	6.6	6.5	6.5
3	13.4	10.9	9.7	8.9	8.4	8.0	7.8	7.6	7.4	7.3	7.2	7.1	7.0	6.9	6.8	6.8
4	13.7	11.2	10.0	9.2	8.7	8.3	8.1	7.9	7.7	7.6	7.5	7.4	7.3	7.2	7.1	7.1
5	14.0	11.5	10.3	9.5	9.0	8.6	8.4	8.2	8.0	7.9	7.8	7.7	7.6	7.5	7.4	7.4
6	14.3	11.8	10.6	9.8	9.3	8.9	8.7	8.5	8.3	8.2	8.1	8.0	7.9	7.8	7.7	7.7
7	14.6	12.1	10.9	10.1	9.6	9.2	9.0	8.8	8.6	8.5	8.4	8.3	8.2	8.1	8.0	8.0
8	14.9	12.4	11.2	10.4	9.9	9.5	9.3	9.1	8.9	8.8	8.7	8.6	8.5	8.4	8.3	8.3
9	15.2	12.7	11.5	10.7	10.2	9.8	9.6	9.4	9.2	9.1	9.0	8.9	8.8	8.7	8.6	8.6
10	15.5	13.0	11.8	11.0	10.5	10.1	9.9	9.7	9.5	9.4	9.3	9.2	9.1	9.0	8.9	8.9

Number of 3 Syll-a-ble words (S)

$$R.A. = 0.3 \left(\frac{100}{N} + 5 \right) + 5$$

Produced by West Lancashire Adult Basic Education Service (Skelmersdale College)

Reading Selections

Selection	Approximate Level
Bob	Basic Literacy
Flying	Post Basic Literacy
First Day at School	Intermediate Level (pre GCSE)
The Amazon Rainforest	Medium (GCSE)
Chumley	Medium (GCSE)
Earthquake	Medium (Post GCSE)
Hooliganism	Medium (Post GCSE)
Everest	Advanced

Bob

When Bob grew up he was just the same. I kept hoping that he would begin to act like a normal person. He didn't. As he got older he got more odd, more crazy.

Bob spent most of his time going from job to job. Sometimes he would stick at a job for a few weeks. Sometimes he left after a few days. No one can live like that for long. You have to get a proper job. You need money to live.

When Bob was very hard up I used to give him a bit of money. Not much. Just a few pounds to keep him going. I felt sorry for him. Bob wasn't like other people. He didn't fit in. He wasn't a layabout. Not really. He was a bit mad. He couldn't help it. He was born that way.

Anyway, Bob was my friend. I had to help him. He didn't have many friends. I was the only person he could go to when he was in trouble.

There was one thing that Bob really loved doing. He loved painting. I don't know much about painting. I was never any good at drawing or painting, but I could tell that Bob was good.

He did lots of paintings. He didn't ever sell them. He didn't make any money out of them. But they were good paintings. Bob put a lot of feeling into them. When I looked at those paintings I felt as if I could understand what was going on in Bob's mind. The paintings seemed to be part of him.

He always did paintings of places. Not real places. Just places he made up. Hills covered with trees. Fields of yellow corn. Yellow corn in the sunshine. Places like that. They were all in Bob's mind. He had never been to a place like that. He lived in the town and he didn't have the cash to go on holiday.

From 'The Ear' by Anita Jackson, reproduced by kind permission of Stanley Thornes Publishers Ltd

Comprehension – Bob

1. Describe, in as much detail as you can remember, the passage you have just read.

....

....

....

2. What happened to Bob as he got older? ....

3. What did Bob do about a job? ....

4. Why did the author feel sorry for Bob? ....

5. What did the author think was good about Bob's paintings? ....

6. What did Bob paint? ....

7. What do you think Bob thought about money? ....

Flying

Afraid of flying? Well – yes and no, I suppose. I've been in a lot of dangerous situations, of course. Over Bolivia, for example. I was working for a small airline, and we carried just about everything, animals, whiskey, dynamite, and, of course, people. There were times when I felt I was flying a bomb, not a plane. Once, I was taking dynamite to the mines. Dynamite! Man, I have never seen so much. They had even put some on the floor right next to me. I was certainly nervous on that trip. Well, I was flying over mountains when suddenly the engine stopped. That time I landed without the plane. I got down all right, but I was hurt. I was lying there for about four days before they found me. They told me later that they had almost given me up for dead. Anyway, they got me back to hospital, and three months later I was flying again. No, I'm not afraid of flying. But there's a lot to worry about as pilot.

You know, flying the big planes over here in Europe isn't really less dangerous than flying those small planes in Bolivia. Near the airports there's such a lot of traffic. Only last week, I had just flown over from New York and was landing at Frankfurt airport. Suddenly I saw a small plane in front of me. It was crossing the airport – right in front of me. There's nothing you can do then, at 150mph. Anyway, I was lucky that time. I hadn't been able to move a finger!

Source unknown

Comprehension – Flying

1. Describe, in as much detail as possible the passage you have just read.

   ....

   ....

   ....

   ....

2. When he worked in Bolivia, what sort of things did they carry?

   ....

3. Where did they put the dynamite?

   ....

4. What happened the time the engine of his plane stopped?

   ....

5. How long was it before he was found?

   ....

6. Was flying in Europe less dangerous than in Bolivia?

   ....

7. What happened at the Frankfurt Airport?

   ....

8. Is this pilot afraid of flying?

   ....

First Day at School

I can remember my first day at the infant school quite well. My mother took me down to the gate of the school, big black iron gates with rust flaking off the bars. There was a huge cedar tree in the grounds, which was propped up by a pair of wooden telegraph poles. I never went too close to it then because I was never quite sure whether telegraph poles were very strong. As we went in, we were greeted by a smell of clay, paint and plimsolls, and earlier I had asked my mother what the rubber toe-caps were for. She said that they were to protect your feet. So as I went into school, I kicked the door frame as hard as I could and discovered to my distaste that they didn't really at all.

Later on, I was taken, with my mother, to see the Headmistress as were all newcomers. Looking out of the window, I saw what I thought was a walking stick on the roof. It turned out to be the top end of a fire-escape ladder.

Then my mother went home and I was taken into a classroom with lots of other little boys and girls, all engaged in painting things or doing things in the sand-pit, or knocking down other people's brick buildings. I found a wooden set of farm animals, and broke the donkey. Our classroom had large windows, with strange things outside. These were 'The Apparatus' which we were to climb on during P.E.

The teacher was a friendly person who showed us where things were and where to get milk. I hated milk. Once I was forced to drink it, or rather the teacher left me the milk with a quarter of an hour to get rid of it. It ended up being poured in the sand-pit.

When it was dinner-time, everyone went home except some of the boys and me. I went off to the dining-hall with the others. We had to go up a sloping corridor called 'The Link' and through a place where there is a notice displayed: 'This is the Quiet Part of the School', and then into the dining-hall. There were rows and rows of trestle-tables and benches. There was a ghastly smell of school dinner type stew and cleaning polish.

After dinner, we did some spelling, and I got my question right which made me most pleased with myself. My mother turned up in the doorway, and I explained to her that plimsolls do not protect your feet, that there was a walking-stick on the roof, and I got about twelve questions right. On the way home I was a dustman because I had my cap on just like dustmen do (back to front). I was proud to be a schoolboy.

Source unknown

Comprehension – First Day at School

1. Describe, in as much detail as you can remember, the passage you have just read.

....

....

....

....

2. Describe the gates of the school.

....

3. What did the boy's mother tell him the rubber toe caps on his plimsolls were for?

....

4. What's the first thing the boy did in the classroom?

....

5. How did he feel about drinking his milk?

....

6. Where did he eat dinner? What did he have?

....

7. What happened during spelling?

....

8. On the way home, how did he pretend he was a dustman?

....

The Amazon Rainforest

My speciality is insects. Ever since I was a boy I was fascinated by insects. A colourful and pretty beetle called 'joanina' (ladybird) was my favourite. I used to capture and collect them. That early boyhood love explains why I chose to become an entomologist, which is a person who studies insects.

As I enjoy catching insects and studying how they live, I'm lucky to be working in the rich Amazon rainforest where about one-third of the world's million or so species of insects live. Because there's a shortage of entomologists in the world, a complete study of the Amazon insects has yet to be done. We still have lots to learn, but our time is running out.

Some scientists say that in a few years time, the forests and jungles of the Amazon region will no longer exist, because they are being so rapidly destroyed by men who are building roads and housing settlements with no thought of protecting the natural habitat.

I am one of a group of about 250 scientists from many parts of the world who work together with Brazilians to research and study the fauna and flora of the Amazon.

A few years ago, when I was working for an examination, I had to observe communities of insects inside the rainforest. I found an old abandoned farm house near a stream and spent one week every month for a whole year working there. I gathered insects, including microscopic ones, from the rocks, tree trunks, fallen leaves, water and sand. Sometimes I had to dive into the streams with a mask and snorkel to find certain species.

One night in this lonely place in the dark jungle, there was a big storm with thunder and lightning. For the first time in my life I was really scared. I felt totally powerless and began to understand why the Indians, who live in the forest, feared these forces of nature and treated them like gods.

Source unknown

Comprehension – The Amazon Rainforest

1. Describe, in as much detail as you can remember, the passage you have just read.

....

....

....

....

2. What is the author's job?.

....

3. What was his favourite insect when he was a boy?

....

4. Where does he work?

....

5. How many species of insects are there in the world?

....

6. Why do some scientists think the Amazon rainforest will soon no longer exist?

....

7. Where did he stay when he was working for an examination?

....

8. What effect did being alone in the jungle storm have on him?

....

Chumley

Chumley was a full-grown chimpanzee. His owner, a District Officer, was finding the ape's large size rather awkward and he wanted to send him to London Zoo as a present, so that he could visit the animal when he was back in England on leave. He wrote asking us if we would mind taking Chumley back with us when we left and depositing him at his new home in London and we replied that we would not mind at all.

He arrived in the back of a small van, seated sedately in a huge crate. When the doors of this crate were opened and Chumley stepped out with all the ease and self-confidence of a film star, I was considerably shaken, for, standing on his bow legs in a normal slouching chimp position, he came up to my waist, and if he had straightened up, his head would have been on a level with my chest. He had huge arms, and must have measured at least twice my measurements round his hairy chest. Owing to bad tooth growth both sides of his face were swollen out of all proportion, and this gave him a weird pugilistic look. His eyes were small, deep-set, and intelligent. The top of his head was nearly bald owing, I discovered later, to his habit of sitting and rubbing the palm of his hand backward across his head, an exercise which seemed to afford him much pleasure and which he persisted in until the the top of his skull was quite devoid of hair. This was no young chimp as I had expected, but a veteran of about eight or nine years old, fully mature, strong as a powerful man, and to judge by his expression, with considerable experience of life. Although he was not exactly a nice chimp to look at (I had seen more handsome), he certainly had a striking personality: it hit you as soon as you set eyes on him. His little eyes looked at you with great intelligence and there seemed to be a glitter of ironic laughter in their depths that made you feel uncomfortable.

I sat down opposite him and produced a packet of cigarettes. As I was selecting, one long black arm was stretched across the table, and Chumley grunted in delight. Wondering what he would do, I handed him a cigarette, and to my astonishment he put it carefully in the corner of his mouth. I lit my smoke and handed him the matches thinking that this would fool him. He opened the box, took out a match, struck it, lit his cigarette, threw the matches down on the table, crossed his legs again and lay back in his chair inhaling thankfully and blowing clouds of smoke out of his nose.

from 'The Overloaded Ark' by Gerald Durrell, reproduced by kind permission of Faber & Faber Ltd

Comprehension – Chumley

1. Describe, in as much detail as you can remember, the passage you have just read.

   ....

   ....

   ....

   ....

2. Where was Chumley being sent? Why?

   ....

3. Describe Chumley physically.

   ....

4. Describe Chumley's personality.

   ....

5. Why was Chumley bald?

   ....

6. How old was he?

   ....

7. Describe the incident with the cigarettes.

   ....

8. What things about Chumley surprised the author?

   ....

Earthquake

The earthquake had done little to clear the air. It was as hot as ever. In the animal world there seemed some strange commotion, as if they had wind of something. The usual lizards and mosquitoes were still absent; but in their place the earth's most horrid progeny, creatures of darkness, sought the open; land-crabs wandered about aimlessly, angrily twiddling their claws; and the ground seemed almost alive with red ants and cockroaches. Up on the roof the pigeons were gathered, talking to each other fearfully.

It was the custom that, whenever their father had been to St. Anne's, John and Emily should run out to meet him, and ride back with him, one perched on each of his stirrups.

That Sunday evening they ran out as soon as they saw him coming, in spite of the thunderstorm that by now was clattering over their heads – and not only over their heads either, for in the tropics a thunderstorm is not a remote affair up in the sky, as it is in England, but it is all round you; lightning plays ducks and drakes across the water, bounds from tree to tree, bounces about the ground, while the thunder seems to proceed from violent explosions in your own very core.

'Go back! Go back, you damned little fools!', he yelled furiously; 'Get into the house!'

They stopped, aghast; and began to realise that after all it was a storm of more than usual violence. They discovered that they were drenched to the skin – must have been the moment they left the house. The lightning kept up a continuous blaze; it was playing about their father's very stirrup-irons and all of a sudden they realised he was afraid. They fled to the house, shocked to the heart and he was in the house almost as soon as they were. Mrs Thornton rushed out:

'My dear, I'm so glad . . .'

'I've never seen such a storm! Why on earth did you let the children come out?'

I never dreamt they would be so silly! and all the time I was thinking – but thank Heaven you're back!'

'I think the worst is over now'.

Perhaps it was; but all through supper the lightning shone almost without flickering. And John and Emily could hardly eat; the memory of that momentary look on their father's face haunted them.

Source unknown

Comprehension – Earthquake

1. Describe, in as much detail as you remember, the passage you have just read.

....

....

....

....

2. What had happened as a result of the earthquake?

....

3. How were the animals affected?

....

4. Where does the story take place?

....

5. What are the children's names?

....

6. Why was their father angry?

....

7. How was this storm different from others?

....

8. What scared the children most?

....

Hooliganism

Undoubtedly the most damaging aspect our our football at the moment is hooliganism. Other facets of the matter may be debated; this violence is solely harmful. Mr Dennis Follows, when he was secretary of the Football Association, diagnosed it accurately when he advocated the banning of spectators under the age of eighteen from football grounds.

His idea was rejected for valid human reasons. Saturday has replaced the old Sunday morning as the working man's time of glory. The football match, core of Saturday, is, for many orderly youthful citizens as well as the unruly, the compensation for a week of monotonous, depressing work and, often, dispiriting family life. Mr Follows identified the specifically disruptive adolescent element.

On the other hand, many of his critics appeared to think that the youngsters in question were simply football followers enthusiastically supporting their own teams. If that were the whole matter it would be relatively easy to adjust; but it is not. Apparently it is not generally realized that many of these young men drink heavily on their football match 'day out'. The youngest of them – quite early teenagers – can be seen buying drink in the public-houses near many of the large grounds; it is simpler, safer, and more profitable for publicans to serve them than to ask their age or refuse. It may be accepted from one who has now twice been forced to defend himself against their mindless violence, that a mob of drunken fifteen or sixteen-year-olds is frighteningly illogical, unpredictable, and potentially violent.

A significant statistic of public reaction shows that in a recent year Boxing Day attendances at League matches were 300,000 lower than in the previous year. This, on a fine day for the season, could not be explained away by the postponement of one Second and one Fourth Division match, the general quality of play, or competition from television.

The effect of hooliganism is almost certainly wider than has generally been accepted. It is not limited to driving away spectators who used to watch from the terraces, who are not prepared to take the risk of violence there, but cannot afford grandstand seats. It is increasingly clear that a considerable number of people, who used to travel by train to 'their' team's away matches or from areas without first-class football, no longer do so because of the atmosphere created by young supporters in trains and at railway stations.

Source unknown

Comprehension – Hooliganism

1. Describe, in as much detail as you remember, the passage you have just read.

....

....

....

....

2. Who is, or was, Dennis Follows?

....

3. What did he advocate?

....

4. Why was his idea rejected?

....

5. What is the problem?

....

6. Why don't publicans refuse to serve the young men?

....

7. What is public reaction to hooliganism?.

....

8. What statistic does the author quote?

....

9. What other effects of hooliganism have there been?

....

Everest

The rarefied air surrounding the upper part of Everest, or any other of the big peaks, obviously makes movement, even over easy ground, much more difficult. Lack of oxygen also slows down and blurs the mental processes. Beyond a certain point life itself is no longer possible. On the other hand, it is now sufficiently proved that the ill-effects of altitude on the climber may at least be retarded by a careful regimen of what we call acclimatization, a gradual getting used to increased height over a certain period of time. Individual performances on a mountain naturally vary but it may be said that those among us who are best adapted to climb high mountains, provided they follow this policy of gradualness, can reach an altitude of at least 21,000 feet and remain there without serious detriment – at any rate long enough to make a supreme final effort to reach a higher point, provided it is not too far above.

Trouble begins above that height, which is one main reason why the really high peaks – those of 26,000 feet and over – are in a different category of difficulty from any lesser ones. The policy of gradualness breaks down, for the muscle tissues begin to deteriorate fairly rapidly and the climber's resistance to cold, his fortitude in the face of wind and weather, are weakened. He tends to lose the promptings of appetite and thirst and he is denied the relaxation of normal sleep. In fact, from about 21,000 feet onwards, he really needs greatly to speed up the rate of his progress and employ 'rush' tactics. But this he cannot do. On the contrary, he is increasingly handicapped by the height as he climbs and his progress becomes painfully slow; the mental effort, like the physical, is infinitely greater. If this is true of easy ground, it is the more so when difficulties arise, even minor ones which would not deter a moderate performer at a lower height. A slight change of gradient may be a straw which will break the camel's back. Considering that Everest is over 29,000 feet and that some 8,000 feet have to be climbed above this established level of successful acclimatization, one aspect of our problem, which also played an important part in defeating former expeditions, becomes clear.

from 'The Ascent of Everest' by Sir John Hunt, reproduced by kind permission of Hodder & Stoughton Ltd

Comprehension – Everest

1. Describe, in as much detail as you can remember, the passage you have just read.

....

....

....

....

2. Why is movement on the upper part of Everest more difficult?

....

3. What is acclimatization?

....

4. Why does a climber acclimatize himself?

....

5. At what height does trouble begin for a climber?

....

6. What happens to a climber beyond this height?

....

7. What should a climber do to achieve the climb?

....

8. What explanation does the author give for why former expeditions have been defeated?

....

Appendix IV

The Irregular Word List

ache	placebo
debt	facade
psalm	gauche
chord	banal
bouquet	deny
heir	equivocal
aisle	quadruped
subtle	nausea
superfluous	naive
zealot	thyme
aeon	courteous
gaoled	hiatus
gist	simile
rarefy	procreate
cellist	gouge

The Long Regular Word List

adventurously	chitterling
individual	herpetology
uninterested	fleeringly
experimenter	huckaback
apprehensive	intertergal
indiscoverable	tipularian
manufactured	gressorial
organisations	pegmatitic
particularly	hectographic
masterpiece	shibboleth

Nelson, Hazel E. 'New Adult Reading Test', Test Manual 1977

The Snowling Graded Nonword Reading Test (Revised Pilot Version)

Name ....

Practice Samples

fer ....   mot ....

wut ....   kib ....

hin ....

One-syllable items

1. mosp ....   6. gromp ....

2. kisp ....   7. snid ....

3. drant ....   8. hast ....

4. prab ....   9. trolb ....

5. sted ....   10. twesk ....

Two-syllable items

1. hinshink ....   6. tegwop ....

2. molsmit ....   7. balras ....

3. nolcrid ....   8. chamgalp ....

4. twamket ....   9. kipthirm ....

5. stansert ....   10. sloskon ....

Observations

....

....

....

Score

One syllable ....

Two syllable ....

courtesy of Dr Margaret Snowling, the updated version is due to be published by the author, 1993

Appendix V

Spelling Dictation Example

Diagnostic Three

(may be suitable for children in Year 5 – P5 in Scotland)

One night my friend woke me, saying, 'Would you enjoy a trial run in my new helicopter?' I had scarcely scrambled into my tracksuit before we were away. The lights of the city glowed beneath, and the stars shone above. I was beginning to wonder about our destination. Then I caught sight of the spinning knife edge and the surface of a flying saucer whistling round. We dodged skilfully in order to avoid an accident. To our relief, the spacecraft regained height and we sank down to earth. I woke in my comfortable bed which I had never actually left.

from 'Spelling in Context' by Margaret Peters and Brigid Smith, reproduced by kind permission of NFER-NELSON Publishing Company Ltd.

Diagnostic dictations level 1, 2 and 4 can be found in 'Spelling in Context' by Margaret Peters and Brigid Smith.

Appendix VI

Advanced Spelling List

intelligible	temporarily
innumerable	curiosity
unconscionable	convenience
antecedent	conveyance
acquittal	abstinence
occurrence	catastrophe
sarcasm	beneficial
righteous	luxuriate
illustration	typhoid
triumph	pageant
deprecate	intrusion
personnel	visibility
compensatory	tyrannical
courtesy	remunerative